FOR BETTER,
FOR WORSE,
for keeps

God's gift of hope for every marriage

by Bob and Cheryl Moeller

MARRIAGE
VINE
PUBLISHING

© 2006 by
Bob and Cheryl Moeller

FOR BETTER, FOR WORSE, FOR KEEPS
God's Gift of Hope for Every Marriage

Originally published by Multonmah Books,
© 1993 Robert Moeller.

Published by MarriageVine Publishing
a division of MarriageVine, Inc.

MarriageVine Publishing books may be purchased in bulk for educational, business, fundraising, or sales promotional use. For information, please email resources@marriagevine.com or visit www.MarriageVine.com

Scripture taken from the HOLY BIBLE, NEW INTERNATIONAL VERSION®. NIV®. Copyright© 1973, 1978, 1984 by International Bible Society. Used by permission of Zondervan. All rights reserved.

ISBN: 0-9786902-0-6
ISBN 13: 978-0-9786902-0-5

MarriageVine Publishing
www.MarriageVine.com

1 3 5 7 9 10 8 6 4 2

Printed in the United States of America

To our six children,
who mean more to us than life itself.
And to our parents,
who taught us a lesson beyond value —
never give up.

Table of Contents

Acknowledgements..7

Foreward...9

Preface..13

PART ONE

1. Not According to Plan..15
2. Checking In at Heartbreak Hotel:
    Where Did Our Marriage Go Wrong?......................................21
3. Searching for the Escape Clause...37
4. If You Keep Your Vows, They'll Keep You..............................55

PART TWO

5. Repairing Your Marriage..75
6. Communication Is the Key...89
7. Aren't My Needs Your Needs?..101
8. Making War, Not Love..109
9. You Can't Have It All..119
10. Sexual Magnetism in Marriage...129

PART THREE

11. The Higher and Hidden Purposes of God..............................147
12. Playing for Keeps...161

Notes...173

Acknowledgements

We have met "agents of grace" in Rick Pierce and his wife, Laura, the founders and leaders of MarriageVine, a growing and fruitful ministry to marriages throughout the nation. We were first introduced to Rick when he began coordinating marriage conferences for us with Moody Bible Institute well over a decade ago. Now, in more recent days we have begun a new partnership with him and MarriageVine.

It was Rick's initiative and vision to revise and update *For Better, For Worse, For Keeps*, our first book on marriage. Through his wise counsel, tireless energy, and candid feedback what was just once a hope has now become a reality.

So, Rick, we wish to publicly thank God for bringing you and your wife into our lives once again, and pray that you will both be richly rewarded for being channels of grace. You bring to mind Paul's words of gratitude to his friend Philemon, "For we have great joy and encouragement in your love, because the hearts of the saints have been refreshed by you, brother." (Philemon 7)

We cannot say it any better than that.

Bob and Cheryl

Foreward

Many years ago I took my first full time job at a small college where I taught psychology and counseling courses. One day the director of a school choir asked if my wife and I could accompany the group on their spring tour. For a couple of weeks we visited a different church every night where the choir presented their concert and I gave a little talk about the school. Following each concert my wife and I usually went to the pastor's home where we would drink coffee and almost always talk about the challenges of ministry, including the difficulties of pastoral counseling. Repeatedly those pastoral couples would tell us about the marriage and family issues that the people in their congregations faced. So many people were having trouble getting along as families, struggling to keep their marriages together, coping with abuse and violence in the home, dealing with alcoholism, trying to have better sex, or wanting guidelines for being better parents. It seemed like every night the pastor or the pastor's spouse would ask if I had ever considered writing a book, bringing my psychological training into a format that could be applied to the church. Perhaps more than anything else, God used those late night discussions to nudge me into writing. I have been writing or editing books ever since.

I soon discovered that thousands of books get published every year. Undoubtedly there are thousands of others that are written but never published. Of the ones that get published, most sell a few thousand copies and soon disappear from the shelves of the publishers or the book sellers. Only the better books keep going. Only a few get revised and are worth getting published again. This is one of those books. It is an updated and expanded version of an earlier book, put into language that fits the twenty-first century, but dealing with the ongoing topics of marriage, family and sexuality that I heard about in those pastoral homes so many years ago.

I first met Bob Moeller when we worked at Trinity Divinity School. Shortly thereafter I met Cheryl and got to know them better when we worshipped for several years at the same church. Even then it was clear to me that Bob is a gifted speaker, a devoted husband, a committed family man, and an effective communicator with an ability to write clearly and competently. Cheryl is an engaging speaker and dedicated believer, deeply committed to her marriage. For twenty five years she has put career aspirations aside so she could focus on raising their six children as a "stay-at-home-mom" with an ability to laugh at the challenges, even as they are treated seriously.

Over the years our families lost track of each other but recently I discovered that we live in the same community now. In looking at this revised edition of the book I was reminded again that this is a book that draws on the rich experiences of a pastor, editor, counselor, and public speaker. Bob freely brings in his own counseling experiences, humorously shares his own foibles, gives a variety of case histories, and points us to biblical illustrations of marriages that have faced tough times and come through difficulties. Cheryl brings her own commitment to writing, her sense of humor, and her experiences in raising an active family. Like its earlier versions this book is interesting, well written, useful, and filled with practical benefits. It can be relevant for anyone who is contemplating marriage or trying to keep a marriage alive, personally and sexually fulfilling, and renewed during times when marriages seem under increasing pressure.

Books on marriage continue to appear, largely because couples have so many stresses and because even good marriages are hard to keep alive and growing. In the midst of this flood of printed and other materials I hope that many people will reach for this book like an old friend that can offer sage and helpful advice. Like so many who have read the earlier editions, I suspect you will find this to be a book that is entertaining, thought-provoking, and genuinely helpful. I am happy to recommend it.

Gary R. Collins, Ph.D.
Clinical psychologist,
author of *Christian Counseling: A Comprehensive Guide*

Preface

We wish one book could cover all the vital areas of distress and problems that can occur in a marriage, but it's simply not possible. *For Better, For Worse, For Keeps* deals with the more common and negotiable problems in marriage. We urge those with more complex marital problems (particularly those individuals whose spouses are chemically dependent, unfaithful, emotionally or physically abusive, or who evidence disruptive emotional, spiritual, or psychological problems) to seek competent professional help immediately.

Let us also say a word about the illustrations and stories in this book. They are based on actual situations, or the composite of several individuals and situations. No story or illustration is unique to one person or couple. In each case we have seen more than one example of the type of problem or situation we describe in order to include it in the book. The names, locations, and circumstances have been significantly altered to protect identities. The problems and difficulties of marriage are so common and universal that some similarities to our own experiences are bound to occur. Solomon was right when he observed, "There is nothing new under the sun."

Finally, it's important to remember the purpose of this book is to offer couples hope, not guaranteed solutions. Ultimately, it's up to us as husbands and wives to seek out the answers we need, to invest the necessary time and energy to solve issues, and to commit ourselves to the hard work and sacrifices required to build a lasting and loving relationship.

That is the adventure of marriage.

PART ONE

Chapter One

NOT ACCORDING
TO PLAN

MARTIN AND HELEN HAVE BEEN MARRIED nearly forty years. To outsiders, their marriage would appear to be a success, but not everything is as appearances suggest. Early in their marriage Martin wanted to go overseas and teach English in a two-thirds world country. Helen resisted the idea, citing health concerns, poor pay, and the lack of good schools for the children. To accommodate his wife, Martin reluctantly gave up his dream and has spent his career in a civil service position instead.

Today he finds himself struggling with anger and resentment toward her. He seems obsessed with the past, imagining what life could have been like if he had not listened to her. "If only," he says day after day to himself. "If only I had followed my heart."

Ryan and Whitney have been married just seven years. Ryan comes home from work one day and finds the house strangely quiet. When he walks up to their bedroom, he discovers Whitney's closet is empty. Bewilderment soon gives way to panic and Ryan begins furiously searching the house for some clue to what has happened. In his hunt, he at first misses the obvious – a note pinned to a throw pillow on the bed. Trembling, he picks it up and scans its contents.

"Dear Ryan, this is the hardest thing I've ever done in my entire life. But it's the only way I know to get your attention. I've been trying to tell you for a long time that I couldn't go on with things the way they are. But you wouldn't listen. Maybe now you will. Don't try to contact me. Right now I just need space. Love, Whitney."

No one sees Ryan for two days. He doesn't even call in sick at work. He just sits in the living room by himself, unable to react.

Campbell and Janáe are on the third day of their honeymoon in the

Caribbean. Seated on the balcony of their hotel room overlooking the crystal green ocean and coral white beaches, Janáe believes it is the ideal setting for love. But Campbell is unusually quiet. "What's wrong, dear?" she asks, reaching out for his hand.

Campbell feigns a smile. "Nothing, sweetheart."

"No, really, something's bothering you. Please tell me what it is."

Campbell looks away, a pained expression on his face. He is silent for a long while and then turns toward his new bride. "Janáe, I've been struggling the last few days."

"With what?"

"I'm not sure..." he hesitates, trying to decide if he should say what is on his heart. Finally he takes the plunge. "I...I'm not sure if I should have married you. I don't know if I love you or not."

Janáe stares at her new husband for a moment, trying to absorb the shock of what she has just heard. Then, without a word, she gets up from the table and runs inside. Even though she closes the door behind her, Campbell can hear the muffled sobs coming from the bathroom. He feels awful, awful for what he has just said, awful because it's true. But with this difficult confession he has experienced a certain relief. At last his agony is no longer a secret.

FROM PASSION TO PAIN

What do these three stories have in common? They're stories of marriages that have gone from "for better" to "for worse." They're examples of people who need to learn to love each other again and to discover that God's plan for their lives includes the person they married "for keeps."

Many people believe that lifetime love is only for the lucky or the strong. It's not. God's design for marriage is for every couple to know true intimacy, deep fulfillment, and the exhilarating experience of being loved just for who they are.

Yet, the design for marriage and the reality of marriage often don't match. Each year millions of couples choose divorce, adultery, or an armed truce as a means of coping with a disappointing marriage. But it doesn't have to be that way.

For Better, For Worse, For Keeps is a book about hope—hope for couples who have watched their marriages go from a passionate love affair to a daily drudgery, or even worse. But it isn't a book just for marriages on the brink. It is for any couple who desires to renew their love and commitment to their marriage. Hope, love, grace, a fresh start, a second chance—these are the essential elements of renewing a marriage when the going gets tough.

An experience I (Bob) had in high school might serve as a useful analogy. I was earning extra money at the time by working nights as a janitor in the Department of Agriculture building. Besides cleaning bathrooms and emptying wastebaskets, I was assigned a highly critical task: buffing the tile floors on the perimeter of the office complex. You may not be familiar with what a buffing machine looks like. It resembles an upright vacuum cleaner with handlebars and a giant circular disk on the bottom the size of a manhole cover. As the disk spins around at the speed of light it polishes the floor.

Using only one finger, the foreman demonstrated the relative ease of operating this high-powered machine. He slid the machine effortlessly back and forth across the tile. Together, he and the buffing machine resembled an Olympic figure skating pair, gliding on ice, responding in perfect synchronization to each other's moves.

"There they go, Janet. This is the last move in the compulsories. They're going to attempt a double axle. Yes! They've done it! A perfect 10!"

"Do you think you can handle it?" the foreman asked.

"Piece of cake," I replied.

"Good. I have to leave early tonight, so it's your job to do the entire floor by nine o'clock."

As the foreman waved good night, I swaggered up to the machine like John Wayne approaching his horse. I grabbed both handles, closed my eyes, and squeezed the trigger. The machine bolted away from me like a crazed Doberman Pinscher on a short leash.

I desperately tried to hang on as the machine careened from one side of the hallway to the other. It would bang into one wall and then dart off for the other side. As the night wore on, I was repeatedly punched in the stomach by the handlebars, thrown into the wall by the centrifugal force of the disk, and dragged down the hallway. I consoled myself with the Russian proverb, "Every beginning is hard." In this case it was brutal.

As the clock approached nine, I was frantic to finish. I came to the section of hallway outside the head supervisor's office (the Grand Poobah of the Agriculture Department). By now I had managed to gain some control over the buffing machine, and my internal injuries weren't life-threatening. Taking the machine firmly by the handlebars, I determined I would emerge the victor over the buffer or die trying. Steeling myself for the attack, I grabbed it with both hands and hit the switch. This time the machine glided quietly across the floor like a cowed puppy.

"That's more like it. Now we see who's boss," I smirked.

But the machine had only been toying with me to lull me into a trap. As soon as we reached the doorway of the supervisor's office it leaped from the floor onto his carpet (a move it had been planning all along). I stood helpless, unable to react as the buffing machine whirred round and round, driving all the dirt, wax, and foreign particles from the hallway deep into the plush pile of the chief executive's carpet. I may be the only custodian in the history of the Department of Agriculture to have buffed the boss's rug. Stunned by the surprise attack, I retreated from the office before I could do any further damage, dragging the machine with me.

The next day I came to work prepared to pick up my last paycheck. As I approached the foreman, a grin crept across his face. "I see you had a little problem last night."

"I guess it got away from me," I mumbled.

"Don't worry. I cleaned it up before work this morning. The supervisor doesn't know anything about it. You'll get the hang of it."

GRACE: DON'T LEAVE HOME WITHOUT IT

For reasons I still don't understand I was given a second chance at the Department of Agriculture when really I didn't deserve one. That's the nature of grace.

You may have been pummeled, punched, and dragged down the hallway by the disappointments in your marriage. The fabric of your relationship may be marred by deep, ugly, and stubborn memories. You may be all but certain it's over. That's where the power and strength of your vows can carry you through the tough times you're facing. You can learn to love again.

Your promises to each other can put your marriage back on track. But to turn "for worse" into "for better" you will need to give and receive grace from one another. You will need to put the past behind and allow love to be rekindled. You will need to go beyond disappointment and seek the beauty and reality of true intimacy. Fortunately, God is in the business of grace and will help you each step of the way.

A friend of ours was going through a difficult phase in his marriage when he came home one day to find the oak coat rack standing in the middle of the hallway. His wife had covered it with yellow ribbons and placed on it a note that read, "Who cares if it's not a real oak tree? Any old oak tree will do. I love you." His encounter with her unconditional love was a breakthrough. From that day on, their marriage started to change, for better.

In preparation for this book, we spent considerable time researching the popular advice on marriage given in our culture. Some advice we found helpful, some questionable, and some downright absurd. However, the more serious research done on marital relationships confirms one important fact: A person's best hope for experiencing happiness and fulfillment in marriage is to stay with the same partner for a lifetime.[1] Which leads me to agree with Ralph Waldo Emerson, who observed, "The only way out is through." There is no simple way out of the difficulties and tough times you may be facing at the moment. But there is a way through, a way that leads to greater happiness and contentment. Helping couples find that way through is the purpose of this book.

May God be with you as you seek that higher route.

Chapter Two

CHECKING IN AT HEARTBREAK HOTEL:

Where Did Our Marriage Go Wrong?

SUSAN WAS A SWEET, RATHER ORDINARY looking young woman who had never had a steady boyfriend until she met Scott. She wasn't all that attracted to him but was flattered by his romantic attention. If nothing else, his companionship kept her from sitting home alone on Saturday nights.

As time went on, Scott's interest in Susan became more serious. When he finally proposed, she wasn't sure what to do. Although they had been dating for quite a while, Scott was hardly the man of her dreams. He had a dependent personality and was a chronic complainer. Still, Scott was a man, and this might be her only opportunity to get married. So against her better judgment, she said yes.

Did she really love him? That thought troubled her as she picked out china, drew up the guest lists, and asked friends to serve as bridesmaids. *I can learn to love him after we're married,* she would tell herself. *After all, I won't have any choice then.*

When Susan's doubts about Scott would return, she would think back to the difficult days in high school and college when the phone was silent, weekends were long and lonely, and prom nights came and went without her. She never wanted to be that alone again.

Susan successfully managed to keep her anxieties in check until the day of her wedding. Standing at the rear of the church, adorned in white, holding a beautiful bouquet in her hands, she looked down the aisle—and froze. It was as if her subconscious pulled off the gag she had been using to silence it for so long.

What am I doing here? she thought to herself. *I don't love Scott. I'm not even sure I like him.* Seeing him standing at the front of the church suddenly made her feel sick. No rationalization would silence her fears now. *Why am I going through with this?* her mind screamed.

Desperate, she began glancing at the doors, the exit signs, the stairwells—anywhere that might provide an escape from the building. But then another thought seized her. *What would my parents think? What would the guests say if I refused to go through with this? Imagine the embarrassments if I ran out of the church.* Her heart was pounding, and her thoughts were racing out of control. *Was it all a bad dream?*

As the music began to swell and the crowd rose to its feet, she was overwhelmed by the two hundred faces looking her way. They were waiting for her, smiling and nodding. Could she disappoint them? Her family? Scott?

It's too late; I can't back out now, she thought to herself. *I have to go through with this. I'll work out my doubts about Scott later. Right now, I have to do what everyone's expecting me to do.*

Closing her eyes, with her legs threatening to buckle underneath her, she started down the aisle. Feeling as if she was somehow outside her body and simply a spectator to this event, she arrived at the altar, took Scott's hand, and completed the ceremony. It was, in her own words, the worst decision of her life.

Today Susan is troubled, if not obsessed, with the desire to live her life over again. She longs for a chance to turn the clock back just this once. This time she would not marry Scott. This time she'd have the inner strength to leave the church. This time she'd marry someone handsome, sensitive, and romantic. If life would give her just one more chance, she wouldn't make the same mistake twice.

But the clock cannot be turned back. Her wedding day cannot be relived. Because her religious convictions won't allow her to divorce Scott, she's resigned herself to living the rest of her life with a decision she regrets making. She feels trapped.

JACOB AND LEAH'S STORY: IT CAN'T GET WORSE THAN THIS

Susan and Scott are not the first two people on earth to wake up after the wedding and find themselves in a difficult and painful marriage. Unfortunately that same story, with variations in details, happens over and over again every day. In fact, painful as your marriage might be today, we doubt it could be much worse than the story of Jacob and Leah, two people who never had any intention of getting married, but who ended up as husband and wife. Their story offers fascinating insights into the dynamics of a marriage all wrong from day one.

Jacob was born into a family of destiny. His father, Isaac, was the only son of Abraham, the great patriarch of the nation of Israel. God had promised Abraham that all the earth would be blessed through his descendants.

But by rights Jacob's older twin brother, Esau, was set to inherit the family blessing and birthright. Jacob, however, through a series of cunning moves, stole Esau's birthright and the blessing of his father, Isaac.

When Esau realized he had been deceived out of his inheritance by Jacob, he vowed blood revenge. Forced to flee for his life, Jacob ran into the desert in search of a sanctuary. It could have been the end of Jacob, but God had mercy on the young man. Nearly exhausted by heat and thirst, he happened upon a fresh well owned by a shepherd named Laban, who turned out to be his uncle, the brother of his mother Rebekah. Even more remarkable, Laban had a daughter of ravishing beauty—Rachel.

It looked like Jacob's fortunes were changing. In the desert he had found family and a woman who had captured his heart. But Jacob's deceptive lifestyle was about to catch up with him.

What Goes Around, Comes Around

When Jacob asked for Rachel's hand in marriage, Laban rubbed his chin and thought for moment. "I'll tell you what," he said. "Stay and work for me for seven years, and in return I'll give you my daughter's hand."

"Fair enough," Jacob at last responded, casting a glance at the lovely Rachel. The two men shook on it, and for the next seven years Jacob divided his time between grazing sheep and gazing at his fiancé.

Was Jacob anxious to get married? Listen to what happened when the seven years ended:

> Jacob said to Laban, "Give me my wife. My time is completed, and I want to lie with her."
>
> So Laban brought together all the people of the place and gave a feast. But when evening came, he took his daughter Leah and gave her to Jacob, and Jacob lay with her. And Laban gave his servant girl Zilpah to his daughter as her maidservant.
>
> When morning came, there was Leah! So Jacob said to Laban,

"What is this you have done to me? I served you for Rachel, didn't I? Why have you deceived me?"

Laban replied, "It is not our custom here to give the younger daughter in marriage before the older one. Finish this daughter's bridal week; then we will give you the younger one also, in return for another seven years of work.[1]

Jacob couldn't believe it. He had been the victim of an elaborate "sting" operation. Just as Jacob had deceived his brother Esau and his father Isaac, now Laban had done a number on him.

For Jacob to have Rachel, whom he wanted desperately, he had no choice other than to accept his devious uncle's terms. But it would mean working seven more years and spending the rest of his life married also to Leah, a woman he had never had any romantic interest in. Reluctantly, Jacob said yes. The writer of Genesis captures the sad state of affairs between these unwilling partners in just two sentences: "[Jacob] loved Rachel more than Leah. And he worked for Laban another seven years."[2]

The Woman Behind Curtain Number One

How could a story like this happen? How could anyone spend his wedding night with the wrong woman and not notice?

Two explanations have been offered. To begin with, it's possible Jacob had imbibed a bit too much of the fruit of the vine during the wedding festivities. By nightfall he may have been so drunk that he couldn't tell the difference between Leah and Rachel. However, the more likely explanation is that his wife had worn a veil, and it wasn't until the next morning he got a good look at who was behind curtain number one. Once he did, he knew with certainty he didn't like Laban's version of "Deal or No Deal."

Not only did Jacob feel cheated, Leah was also a victim. What should have been a day of celebration turned out to be a day of bitterness. We can only imagine that while Jacob fumed and cursed his bad fortune, Leah wept and grieved over her cruel situation. Few things are more difficult to bear than the knowledge your marriage isn't working and the chances for true love have passed you by.

CHARACTERISTICS OF A MARRIAGE
IN NAME ONLY

Although few modern marriages begin in such a bizarre fashion as Jacob and Leah's did, their story does offer us insights into the traits of marriages that have gone off the track. And when we know where a marriage got off track, we can find ways to restore it.

A Constant State of Misery

Jacob and Leah, though unhappily married, did not live entirely separate lives. They ended up having several children together. The customs of the day demanded that the husband spare his wife the disgrace of a barren womb. So in Jacob and Leah's case, sex was primarily for procreation, rather than as an expression of intimacy or love. To Jacob, fathering children was likely more an obligation than a desire to build a family together. The lack of love in their marriage is evident from the story of the birth of their first child.

Genesis tells us that "Leah became pregnant and gave birth to a son. She named him Reuben, for she said, 'It is because the Lord has seen my misery. Surely my husband will love me now.'"[3] Imagine, Leah named her first son after the word for misery. But ongoing misery is a common characteristic of struggling marriages. Often one spouse lives in perpetual regret for saying, "I do," while the other languishes from lack of love.

Keisha believed she had married beneath her. She was an accountant in a large corporation; her husband Keith was a service sector employee. Even though she had pushed him into marrying her, she resented him from day one. She would walk ahead of him when entering a party. She would publicly scold him for little mistakes he made. She would demand the he "get with it" and find a better paying job. In short, she resented him. As much as he tried to live up to her expectations and improve himself, it didn't work.

Leah knew Jacob didn't love her. That was obvious from the first day of their marriage. She would see Jacob and her sister Rachel disappear into his tent for the night. Imagine the hurt as Jacob would speak tenderly to Rachel in front of the servants, but perhaps ignore or be irritated with Leah. Perhaps Jacob brought gifts for his beloved Rachel and pampered her with clothes, perfumes, and spices, while Leah was given nothing but the necessities of life. Is it hard to imagine why she named her first child "misery"?

Using Children to Try to Save the Marriage

Leah said something significant when Reuben was born: "Surely my husband will love me now." It's typical for couples caught in a sinking marriage to try to remedy their relationship by having a child. One spouse thinks, *If I produce something my mate loves and values, then perhaps he (or she) will love and value me as well.*

Unfortunately, what often happens is that after the baby is born there are three miserable people in a family instead of just two. We've watched many unhappily married couples bring children into the world as a method of solving their marital problems—a solution that virtually never works. (That is, however, by no means a justification for abortion.)

Why doesn't having a baby bring a husband and wife together? First, the child represents the unloved mate. The features, hair color, and smile don't matter. That baby is half someone else, the someone the mate doesn't want to be married to. As Donald Joy points out, fathers who aren't bonded to the mothers demonstrate a low investment in the nurture and care of their infants. They won't change diapers, they won't buy toys, they take very few pictures. Why? Because the child represents a relationship they don't value.

Another reason the baby-making solution doesn't work is the added stress it brings. To an already tense situation add a screaming infant who demands nonstop attention and brings on sleep deprivation. That's a lot for even happily married couples to cope with. We know. We had six children. During the hardest of those years we would actually stare in envy at people in the grocery store who looked as if they had slept eight hours the night before.

Finally, bearing a child won't bring a couple together because a baby can't change the heart of another person. Sadly, the power of selfishness, anger, and revenge overrides even the instinctual love a parent should have for his own flesh and blood.

Leah was hoping that by producing a firstborn son, a highly coveted prize in the Near Eastern culture, Jacob's heart would soften toward her.

It did not.

Public Ridicule and Contempt

Unhappy couples often act out their unhappiness in public. They don't care if other people know they aren't in love or can't even stand each other. They are often so caught up in their self-pity and anger that they lose all sense of discretion.

That was the case with Jacob and Leah. The account of the birth of their second son speaks for itself: "[Leah] conceived again, and when she had given birth to a son she said, 'Because the Lord heard that I am not loved, he gave me this one too.' So she named him Simeon," which probably means "one who hears."'

Word of Laban's deception to marry off Leah to Jacob had no doubt spread throughout the village. Leah believed that word of her loveless marriage had reached even heaven, and she was convinced that only the pity of God had allowed her to bear Simeon, her second child.

Can't you see Jacob in the marketplace, complaining to others about Laban's treachery and his homely wife? If Leah had hoped two sons would awaken love in Jacob, she soon found out otherwise.

Spouses who aren't bonded to their mates will often let others know just how miserable they are. Word spreads, and the unloving spouses may even hope that will cause their mates to make a decision they themselves don't want to make—a decision to end the marriage.

Distance and Detachment

Another characteristic of a marriage off track is aloofness and disinterest. Listen to the account of the birth of Leah's third son: "Again she conceived, and when she gave birth to a son she said, 'Now at last my husband will become attached to me, because I have borne him three sons.' So he was named Levi."[5] Scholars believe the name Levi sounds like the Hebrew word for "attached."

That's often what is lacking in a troubled marriage—a sense of mutual attachment. One or both spouses go through the motions of marriage, but their heads and hearts are elsewhere. They just aren't bonded to each other. Through emotional Morse code they send each other the message, "I may be married to you, but I'm not really bonded to you. There's a part of me I'll never let you have—my heart."

That was Drew's perspective. He was an impulsive person who also tended to be egocentric. He probably married Kali because she came from old money. Or because he was lonely. Or perhaps because he wanted someone to help him start his computer business. In any case, he quickly lost interest in her once they were married.

When he came home at night, he would ignore her. Although Kali was an intelligent, well-educated woman, Drew saw her as his intellectual inferior. So he rarely talked to her, listened to her, or asked her advice. Before long he was spending time with others he considered more of his caliber and class.

Distance and detachment—clear signs of partners who believe they could have done better.

Tortured by the "If Onlys"

Some couples get caught in the syndrome of thinking, "If only I had it to do all over again," or "If only I had married another person," or "If only I had remained single longer."

Autumn and Greg were both products of troubled homes. Their unmet needs drew them to each other, and throughout high school they were inseparable. They walked hand in hand everywhere, oblivious to others, always talking openly of their plans to marry. When they graduated from high school, they did marry, but the delayed fuses from their troubled families of origin were set to go off. After the birth of their first child, the detonation occurred.

As their relationship went from bad to worse, Autumn began to think of the boys she could have dated. What if she had married one of them instead of Greg? All her unhappiness could have been avoided. Rather than focusing on her marriage as she needed to, she put more emotional distance between the two of them.

Couples caught in an unhappy marriage look for relief wherever they can find it. Retracing our life's steps and wishing we had made different choices may provide momentary distraction, but ultimately it does nothing to bring reconciliation. It's an exercise in futility. What is more useless than perpetual regret? It can't change the past, and it handicaps us from facing present or future realities with courage and wisdom.

I Married the Wrong Person

The final common symptom of a distressed marriage is the soul-chilling thought, "I married the wrong person." It's a tragedy beyond words when spouses wake up one morning and decide they are married to the wrong person. Like midmorning humidity in August, their marriage suffocates them. Now all they know is they want out. It doesn't matter how, they just want out.

The Bible hints at several marriages that appear to be a mistake (at least in the eyes of one spouse or both). A classic example is the story of Abigail and Nabal, two people who could not have been more poorly matched. Listen to the brief, but tell-all introduction to the Scripture's version of Beauty and the Beast found in 1 Samuel 25: 1-44: "*His name was Nabal and his wife's name was Abigail. She was an intelligent and beautiful woman, but her husband, a*

Calebite, was surly and mean in his dealings."

Do you ever wonder how two polar opposites find each other? From my own observations such opposites first attract but as life plays out later repel each other. In this case even their names spelled trouble for their marriage. Abigail means "my father is joy" conveying the idea of a positive, upbeat personality, while Nabal means "fool" or "vile person." Do you see the problem developing?

The clash of mismatched personalities reaches its climax when David, the future king of Israel, arrives on their estate property with several hundred exhausted and hungry men. David is on the run from the insane King Saul (who has vowed to kill David if he can find him). All the famished David asks for from Nabal is some leftovers from his great wealth. Once they've eaten something he promises he and his men will go on their way.

So how does Nabal answer the future king of Israel? *"Who is this David…Why should I take my bread and water, and the meat I have slaughtered for my shearers, and give it to men coming from who knows where?"* When David hears his answer he knows he's been "dissed" (disrespected) and orders his men, *"Put on your swords!"* Little does Nabal know it, but he's about to be skewered and put on a rotisserie for his rude, impetuous, and foolish behavior.

Abigail hears about the impending barbeque and quickly prepares a meal for David and his men with microwave speed. She fortunately intercepts David on the road before he and his men can slice and dice her clueless husband, *"May my lord pay no attention to that wicked man Nabal. He is just like his name—his name is Fool, and folly goes with him."*

David is moved by Abigail's eloquent plea and turns back from his murderous plan. So you would think Nabal at this point would be immensely relieved and forever thankful for such a capable and intelligent wife? Wrong. *"When Abigail went to Nabal, he was in the house holding a banquet like that of a king. He was in high spirits and very drunk."*

How many nights must have Abigail laid awake and asked, "How did I ever end up marrying such a loser?" That's a question far too many couples agonize over for days, months, and in some cases for even decades.

THE ROOTS OF TROUBLED MARRIAGES

It's obvious how Jacob and Leah ended up in a marriage neither enjoyed. Their troubles could be traced to Laban's elaborate deception. But there are other, more common, roots that can produce a troubled family tree. Let's look at some of the reasons men and women say "I do," only to end up wishing they had said, "I don't."

I've Lost the Feeling

Couples who marry strictly on the basis of their feelings often find their emotions betraying them. Desperate infatuation turns into deep-seated hostility. As the expression says, "Emotions have no intelligence." Physical passions aren't necessarily connected without rational faculties. We can be completely mesmerized by people with whom we have absolutely nothing in common.

Certainly physical attraction is one element of the mystery of love between a man and a woman, but it is meant to be only a minor movement, not the basis for the entire symphony. As Proverbs so aptly observes, "Charm is deceptive, and beauty is fleeting."[6] That's why couples who marry simply out of physical attraction for one another are usually in for discord once the fascination and infatuation wear off.

Research has revealed that the hormones which produce the warm sensation of being "in love" eventually lose their potency. They wear out. So higher and higher levels of the same hormone are required to produce the same feelings of exhilaration.[7] The conclusion: It will take something other than high-voltage body chemistry to keep a couple together for a lifetime. The hormones that produce a "romantic high" just can't be sustained.

Although this false assumption that love is a rapid heartbeat and flushed face keeps reality shows, the Oxygen Channel, and country music in business, it can prove disastrous for marriages. But there is hope for that type of troubled marriage. It requires giving up the adolescent notion that love is the rush you feel when you see the other person. That rush eventually gives out, but that's where real love just begins.

Too Much, Too Soon

If hormones have no intelligence, they also have no virtue. That is, they can't be counted on to help us make the right moral choice of whom to marry.

Kristine and Jack met at the office. Kristine was tired of living alone and was looking for romance and companionship. Jack seemed to offer just what she wanted, but the price he was asking was quite high.

Kristine had been raised to believe that premarital sex was wrong. She had always planned to wait and save her virginity for her future husband. But Jack, sensing she lacked a strong will, kept up the pressure. Eventually, he wore her down.

They later married, but their relationship was in trouble from day one. Kristine was angry at Jack for the pressure he had put on her to compromise. Jack felt guilty about what they had done and began showing less interest in her sexually.

Couples who are sexually active before the wedding day put obstacles in their path to happiness. Although proponents of premarital sex and cohabitation before marriage claim it improves the chances for a successful marriage, the facts don't support the idea. Couples living together before marriage divorce at a much higher rate than those who do not. Marital satisfaction is greater for those who wait than for those who don't.[8] For a variety of reasons, premarital sexual activity can come back to disrupt a marriage years after the wedding. The best chance for good sex after marriage is no sex before marriage.

Mr. Perfect and Miss Ideal
No Longer Live Here

Couples in love commonly idealize their future partner. In their own minds they reshape the other person to fit their perception of the perfect husband or wife. They typically avoid uncomfortable truths about the other person. Why ruin a perfectly good fantasy with harsh realities?

I've (Bob) counseled couples preparing for marriage who assured me they were perfect for each other. Sensing I have Mr. Perfect and Miss Ideal sitting in front of me, I often throw them a curve ball and ask, "Why don't you two tell me about the worst fight you've ever had?"

That usually leads to a moment or two of silence before one breaks the news to me. "Uh, Bob, we've never had a major fight." Pausing for a moment to glance lovingly in the intended's eyes, he or she finishes the thought by saying, "And we plan to never fight. We're in love." The other person usually nods and smiles dreamily as if to say, "That's right. If you were in love like us, you'd understand what we're talking about." I don't enjoy bursting other people's bubbles, so I proceed gently. "Isn't there anything about the other person you find annoying?"

"Not really," they both giggle.

"Well, if you were to have a fight, what do you think it would be over?" I ask. Again there is a long pause. "I can't think of anything, can you, baby?"

"No baby, I can't either," the other one swoons.

Leaning forward, I say, "It sounds as if you two believe you are perfect for each other. Perhaps you are. But I can't marry you until I find out if you're capable of resolving conflict in your relationship. Let's put this wedding off until you've had your first big fight and we can discuss how you worked it out. Then I can help you determine if you are right for each other."

I've come close to needing the electric shock paddles. The look of incredulity from Mr. Perfect and Miss Ideal defies description.

We're worried about couples who are so caught up in their idealized view of each other that they can't see whom they are actually marrying. When reality hits them, it will hit hard.

What drives people to overlook the character flaws in another person? Often it comes from being raised in a troubled home. When addictions, compulsions, and abusive behavior become a way of life in a home, the children grow into adulthood with huge areas of unmet needs. Nature abhors a vacuum, and so people are driven to fill that void. They turn to romance and relationships to try to fill their need for love and acceptance. Because they so badly want to believe another person can solve their interpersonal problems and give them the intimacy they crave, they refuse to see people as they really are. Chances are, they are simply in love with the idea of love, and they are setting themselves up for on of the rudest shocks of their life.

The In-Laws Treat You Like Outlaws

Steve and Laurie were raised in different Protestant denominations. Though they shared a mutual Christian faith and had reached a common spiritual understanding, Steve's parents were rigidly committed to their church and warned him repeatedly of marrying someone outside the fold. They firmly believed that unless their grandchildren were raised in their own denomination they had no hope for salvation.

At first Steve's parents tolerated Laurie, hoping perhaps that she would join their church. As it became apparent Laurie and Steve had other plans, his parents became increasingly hostile.

The entire matter came to a head one day when Steve and Laurie were having lunch with his parents. After the table was cleared, they all agreed they should discuss wedding plans, but Steve's mother took charge of the conversation. "Laurie," she said, clearing her throat, "we raised Steve to be a faithful member of our church. We understand you were raised to believe somewhat differently than he. We respect your right to believe whatever you wish, but I won't have my grandchildren being born into a church different than ours."

Steve blanched. He had no idea his mother was going to do this. "But, Mom," he interrupted, "Laurie is a Christian."

"Don't interrupt me, son. I'm not finished."

Laurie's face mirrored her anguish. She instinctively knew what was coming next.

"Steve's father and I have had to make a difficult decision. If you two go ahead with this wedding and don't promise that you raise the children in our denomination, we won't be attending the ceremony."

Turning toward Steve's mother, Laurie said, "Mrs. Branson, I couldn't care less if you set foot in the church on our wedding day. If you want to ruin the happiest day of our lives in the name of your religion, then go ahead and do so." Then she stood up, grabbed her purse, and ran out the door, tears streaming down her face.

Steve glared at his mother with a mixture of anger and disbelief, and then without saying a word he followed Laurie out the door. Looking out the window, Mrs. Branson could see the two of them sobbing and holding on to each other.

Problems with in-laws have led more than one couple to the brink of divorce. Sometimes the issues are as minor as giving unwanted "helpful hints" regarding housekeeping, finances, or children rearing. Other times they are more serious. Parents desperately cling to their son and daughter and refuse to give them up. They call constantly, demand attention, or find some way to keep their child committed to them first and foremost. If couples don't draw the proper boundaries with in-laws, the underlying tension and division that result can lead a couple to the point of dissolution.

I Owe It to Them

One of the worst reasons to marry is because we feel we owe it to the other person. But it happens every day. Marriage should be an act of love, based on a clear and reasoned choice, motivated by a desire to give, anchored in the firm and unshakable conviction this is the person we wish to spend the rest of our life with. It isn't an IOU to be paid out because our sexual behavior caught up with us or because we feel sorry for someone and want to rescue him or her. Nor should someone choose to go through with the ceremony simply to please others or to avoid embarrassment.

A popular woman's magazine carried the story of a young woman who got married despite her misgivings because it pleased so many other people. The title of the article, "I Knew My Marriage Was a Mistake—at the Reception," says it all.

Why we are willing to risk an entire lifetime of misery to secure the nodding approval of others is a mystery. But in many cases, engaged individuals feel their fate is sealed and it's too late to back out. The tragic result is that although they go through with the wedding, they don't go through with the marriage. The young woman in this story divorced her husband less than eight months after getting married, but not before she cheated on him, humiliated him before his family, and left him brokenhearted and alone to sort out his life.

So Young, So in Love

Loretta Lynn, the famous country and western performer from the 70's and 80's, was married while she was still a teenager. The story of her painful childhood union was chronicled in the classic movie *The Coal Miner's Daughter*. Her father's only advice to her future husband was not to beat her, which he did anyway.

For many reasons, marrying too young often creates a distressed marriage. The most obvious is that few people are mature enough to handle the incredible demands and pressures of marriage when they're still essentially children. Life is nothing less than an extended struggle, and marriage adds to the pressure. Matrimony is no place for youngsters. The statistics tell us that teenagers who volunteer for marital duty more often than not end up casualties.[9]

Perhaps the most insidious aspect of marrying too early is the perpetual doubt it creates. Savannah married when she was only eighteen. To this day she torments herself by asking, *I wonder if I would have married Hernandez if I had just waited another two years?* She has gone through her entire married life believing she was too young to know what she was doing.

To be fair, we've met some happily married, well-adjusted couples who said "I do" long before they reached the age of twenty-one. They survived the rigors of battle and together became a cohesive team. It can be done. But statistics show it's the exception, not the rule.

CONCLUSION

Like Jacob and Leah it's easy to wake up one day and ask, "I reserved the

Honeymoon Suite, so how did I end up in Heartbreak Hotel?" When disappointments, problems, and despair enter the picture, it's easy to start looking for a way out, any way out. But rather than look for a way to escape, which can create more problems than it solves, it is better to understand what brought you to this point and what can be done to get back on track. As we'll learn later in the lives of Jacob and Leah, the early chapters of a painful marriage are not the entire book.

Chapter Three

SEARCHING FOR THE ESCAPE CLAUSE

ONE SNOWY MIDWEST WINTER'S DAY, Andrew and Isabella came to us for counseling. As we talked with them, we quickly picked up that the Andrew wanted out of the marriage as soon as possible. We both suspected that he had a girlfriend. Isabella, suspected someone else was involved as well, though Andrew denied it.

We went into high gear. We prayed for this family night and day. We pleaded with Andrew to stay. They had four beautiful girls still at home and needed both parents. We gave Andrew biblical counsel from God's Word. We told him what a mistake he was making.

Andrew's only retort was, "The actual wedding vows I said on my wedding day are not in the Bible so I'm not obligated to follow them."

It's human nature to seek exemption from the rules. People who find themselves in unhappy or unfulfilling marriages often start scanning the fine print of their wedding contract to find a quick and painless way out. But such an easy exit doesn't exist, and attempting to walk out on your responsibilities eventually lands you in a prison of your own making.

Sometimes we see in our children this same blame-shifting behavior tendency. As a three year old, our youngest daughter MacKenzie tried to put the blame on others for something she had done. We had just purchased a new leather couch when we discovered the letters "ATMO" drawn on the back in permanent magic marker. They weren't just little doodle letters, they were huge...on our brand new couch! When we asked our precious three year old if she had been drawing on furniture again she replied, "No, Bo did it." We didn't have a child named Bo - at least not one that we remembered having. Now, Bo was our dog - a collie to be exact. When we asked her how Bo drew the letters on the couch because he doesn't have hands, she took the magic marker, put it in her mouth, and began to move up and down tracing letters simulating the crime. Bo was not punished, but was forced to write our Christmas letter the next year—(people are still asking what family do they know with the last name ATMO). It's a common temptation to put the blame elsewhere when really something is our own fault.

What are the more popular "escape clauses" people use as an easy out from the promises they made on their wedding day?

THE BIG "D"

Easy divorce is an idea that gained tremendous popularity just about 40 years ago. That's when states began passing "no fault divorce laws." It used to be if you wanted to get a divorce you had to prove someone was at fault. Essentially these new "no fault" laws removed the burden of having to provide compelling reason to dissolve the marriage contract. So if someone wanted out of a marriage, he or she could get out, no questions asked.

The Rockford Institute, a think tank located in the Midwest, has documented that divorce rates rose dramatically in states that adopted "no fault" laws. Rather than solving the problem of divorce in our society, the laws threw gasoline on the raging fire. Common sense could have predicted the accelerated breakup of marriages. The easier it becomes to break a promise, the more often it will be broken. In the last four decades, families began to come apart.[1]

The very notion of "no fault divorce" was ridiculous to begin with. No-fault divorce makes as much sense as no-fault adultery, no-fault theft, or no-fault slander. We can change the semantics as often as we wish, but divorce is still an unnatural and painful injustice inflicted on another person (even if both people agree to it). It is breaking promises, and no-fault promise breaking is simply not possible.

The people of ancient times, eager to find the fine print escape clause in their marriage vows, once asked Jesus, "Is it lawful for a man to divorce his wife for any and every reason?"

Jesus chose not to deal with technicalities but pointed to the grand purpose and design of marriage. " 'Haven't you read,' he replied, 'that at the beginning the Creator "made them male and female," and said, "For this reason a man will leave his father and mother and be united to his wife, and the two will become one flesh"? So they are no longer two, but one. Therefore what God has joined together, let man not separate."[2] What was he saying about marriage and divorce? It's intended "for keeps." Why? Because of its unique creation.

Can you rip a seamless garment in two without doing permanent damage? Can you hammer a priceless sculpture and maintain its beauty? Can you saw a living organism in two without inflicting enormous pain and suffering? That's why God considers divorce immoral; it destroys in a painful and unnatural manner a special work of His creation intended to last a lifetime. To suggest we humans can do just that for "any" and "every" reason is to devalue what God Himself prized so highly.

That's why claiming that no one should bear any fault for willfully destroying such a precious relationship is close to preposterous. How can we destroy the emotional security of another human being, wipe our hands, and announce, "It isn't my fault"? How can we tear in two the hearts of children by forcing them to choose which parent they will live with and they say, "So what? It's best for everyone involved"? How can we break the most sacred of human vows and say, "Who cares? It was all a mistake."

Yes, But Does It Work?

Let's put aside for the moment the question of whether divorce is moral and approach it from a purely pragmatic viewpoint. Will it accomplish what it's supposed to? Does it bring long-lasting relief from the pain, anxiety, and disappointment that come with an unhappy marriage? Does it offer a new lease on life, giving us the opportunity for a fresh start unhindered by the past?

Richard bought the line that divorce could solve his problems. His smallest mistakes, like spilling coffee or forgetting to pay a bill, would send Samantha into a tirade. When Richard finally grew tired of her temper and nagging, he decided divorce was the ticket out. He could unload Samantha and go shopping for someone who would treat him with more respect.

Right after the divorce was granted, Richard felt relieved. It was like walking out of prison into the sunshine. Now he could go on with his life. Soon, however, he began wrestling with deep bouts of loneliness and sadness. The reality of severing the most intimate bond in his life wasn't as painless and easy as he had imagined.

In an effort to fill that void, he began dating again. Eventually he met Masie. She had recently divorced as well, and both agreed their first spouses had been first-class losers. Their romance took off like a greyhound on a racetrack, and almost immediately they were talking about marriage. When they tied the knot, they believed this was the beginning of a new chapter in their lives.

Before long Richard made a startling discovery. Masie, who had seemed mild-mannered and patient, was capable of violent mood swings as his first wife. She was a perfectionist, tormented by anger and a sense of inferiority, and so Richard again found himself on the receiving end of someone else's rage. He was stunned to realize he had gone through the pain of a divorce only to end up in an identical situation. How could it happen twice?

The answer is quite simple. Richard expected more from divorce than it can deliver. It can change our partners, but it can't change who we are. Richard had assumed the problems in his life were caused exclusively by his spouse. All he had to do was get rid of her, and his problems would exit with her.

Albert Ellis, the distinguished psychologist, developed a list of irrational beliefs that guide the lives of many people. One such belief is that "happiness is dependent upon external circumstances or other people." Richard had fallen for that misconception. He believed divorce would change his external world and clear the way for him to be happy.

Does divorce work? From our observations, and from the testimony of numerous divorced individuals we've worked with, the answer is no. It trades one set of problems for another, with the second set often being far worse.[3]

Is It Better for the Kids?

Parents who are feeling guilty about breaking up their home often rationalize that "it's better for the children this way." They reason that an unhappy marriage, filled with angry glares, slamming doors, and silent meals, is far worse on children than no marriage at all.

Newsweek once devoted a major article to this topic. The article begins with the story of Sara Dadisman: "It was her thirteenth birthday. Even now, two decades later, talking about it is difficult for her. 'It seems as though my mom did it to almost hurt me,' says Dadisman. 'Sometimes I think, Was that real? Did she really do that on my birthday? But I can remember her giving me a present, a Barbie doll or something, and then telling me she and my dad were getting a divorce. I was devastated.'"[4]

Several years ago we were moved as we watched a movie about a boy who hires a lawyer to stop his parents from divorcing. The boy claims he is "a necessary party" to the marriage contract and, as such, should be consulted before a divorce is granted. His sister, so traumatized by her parents' separation, begins wearing earmuffs in the middle of summer to keep from hearing any more painful news.

When the case is finally heard in court, the boy argues successfully that there is no compelling reason for his parents' marriage to end. Listening to their son's pleas, the parents are moved to reconsider their decision to destroy their home and their children's happiness.

The final scene of the movie shows the boy and his sister walking down a sidewalk together.

"Do we still have a family?" she asks.

"We still have a family," he replies.

Rigging the Jury against Future Happiness

Clair Bergman, author of *Adult Children of Divorce Speak Out*, says poignantly, "A hole in the heart is universal. There is a sense of having missed out on something as a birthright, the right to grow up in a house with two parents."[5]

We have many friends who were utterly devastated by their parents' divorce. Even after they were grown and married, most never fully recovered from the shock. A sense of invalidation lingers. It's as if they say, "The very union that brought me into existence is broken."

Not only does divorce leave children with track marks across their heart, it rigs the jury against their having a successful marriage later in life. *Newsweek* discovered this significant trend:

> Compared with people who have grown up in intact families, adult children of divorce are more likely to have troubled relationships and broken marriages. A desire for stability sends them down the aisle at too young an age, and they wind up in divorce court not long afterward. Others fear commitment because they learned too well the lesson of their childhood – don't trust anyone, not even Mom or Dad. Even when divorce releases children from their parents' violent or emotionally abusive marriage, they worry that they don't know how to be half of a happy couple because they've never seen one close up at home.[6]

Despite a thousand and one reasons to end a marriage, the emotional need of children to have two parents refutes them all. You may find a different husband or wife, but your kids will never find another mother or father. Parents who truly love their children will give them the gift that only they can offer—

a stable and loving marriage. That's why kids will blush and turn away when they see their parents kiss. They're embarrassed with delight. Each display of affection ties one more rope of security around their heart.

Popular magazines suggest that after decades of a social experiment in human tragedy, even the so-called experts are rethinking their attitude toward divorce. If the cure doesn't work and causes more pain and suffering than the disease, perhaps it's time to switch treatments. Just because your parents divorced doesn't mean you have to divorce.

GIVING A TRYST A TRY

The second most common escape clause that unhappy and unfulfilled spouses try is an affair. It seems to offer the best of both worlds. You can keep your current husband or wife and yet enjoy the thrill of a new love. You get the wild, unrestrained passion of a honeymoon without the hassle of clogged sinks, strep throat, or afternoon carpools. It seems to offer the "for better" without the "for worse."

To be honest, few people sit down and say to themselves, "I think I'll break my wedding vows and have sex with a person I'm not married to." Affairs usually begin much more subtly. People find themselves with unresolved emotional pain or unmet needs. Their spouse is either unaware of what's going on or is unconcerned. Over time, the hunger for intimacy—although initially not in a sexual sense—begins to grow.

Then comes the opportunity. Someone at work, or next door, or even at church begins to show common courtesy and respect. This person is also feeling unfulfilled, and the illusion of intimacy draws the two together.

David Seamands, a well-known marriage counselor and author, tells about counseling a woman caught up in an affair she wanted to end. To help her break the emotional tie to her illicit lover, Seamands told her to bring all the tokens of their relationship and throw them away. He had expected her to hand over a DVD of a romance movie, a love letter, or perhaps even expensive jewelry. Instead, she produced a daily devotional book, *My Utmost for His Highest.* "Don't ask any questions," she said, dropping the book on his desk. If the marriage isn't meeting the spouses' spiritual, emotional, or physical needs, and they start scanning the horizon for a solution, they become prime candidates for adultery.

It can happen to almost anyone. The author of the majority of the book of Psalms was King David of Israel. He is described in the Bible as a man "after God's own heart." He was a courageous warrior, a powerful ruler, and a passionate poet. Yet the Bible records that he committed adultery, had the woman's husband murdered, and then tried unsuccessfully to cover up the whole affair. He suffered the consequences of his foolish behavior for the rest of his life, as his children warred with one another and eventually tried to topple him from his throne. The decline of David's otherwise prosperous and successful life can be traced to the night he spent with Bathsheba.

Is an Affair Good for a Marriage?

Many in our society believe that an occasional fling with another person actually helps a marriage. Advocates of "open marriage" have suggested that couples be free to engage in sexual relationships with others as they choose. That takes the pressure off the mates to be the exclusive provider for their needs.

What's wrong with occasionally straying to enliven a boring and stale marriage? Isn't monogamy a quick ticket to monotony?

To begin with, sex is more than a biological act. It is the union of two people on a physical, emotional, and spiritual level. No human act involves the totality of a person like sexual intercourse. That's why it is to be reserved exclusively for our lifelong mate. The ancient book of Proverbs recognized this truth. "Drink water from your own cistern, running water from your own well. Should your springs overflow in the streets, your streams of water in the public squares? Let them be yours alone, never to be shared with strangers."[7]

The writer was saying nothing is more private, intimate, and exclusive than your sexual identity. Don't cheapen and denigrate who you are by sharing it "with strangers."

The results of a society that has chosen to ignore this advice are frightening. Josh McDowell, who has studied adolescent sexual behavior, recently stated there are now over fifty varieties of sexually transmitted diseases. That's an increase of several fold from just thirty years ago.

Health officials quietly acknowledge there is no "safe sex' outside of a lifetime monogamous relationship. Condoms have at best a 10 percent failure rate, and the HIV virus can potentially be spread simply through the perspiration present in the genital area during intercourse. In other words, if you want to place yourself in the lowest possible risk group of contracting the fatal disease, "Drink water from your own cistern, running water from your own well."[7]

But it is not only the physical dangers adultery poses that should cause people to rethink their behavior. It is the personal, psychological, and relational damage that infidelity causes as well.

Can You Scoop Fire into Your Lap?

Adultery has a curious way of destroying everyone who gets involved in it. How many governors, public officials, and prime ministers have been brought down in shame when their private lives revealed moral compromise? How many pastors, evangelists, and media celebrities have been forced from the pulpit due to infidelity? How many millions of marriages have been irretrievably ruined because a man or woman broke the promise to "forsake all others"? Proverbs asks the question, "Can a man scoop fire into his lap without his clothes being burned? Can a man walk on hot coals without his feet being scorched? So is he who sleeps with another man's wife; no one who touches her will go unpunished."[8]

Sexual innocence is one item given in equal amounts to each man and woman. It can be preserved or squandered, but once it is lost, it is lost forever.

As appealing as adultery might seem to a person in a difficult marriage, it is absolutely the wrong choice. The only freedom it offers is the right to leave your integrity and reputation behind and to endure the disappointment and reproach of those who have trusted you the most. Solomon wrote, "A man who commits adultery lacks judgment; whoever does so destroys himself. Blows and disgrace are his lot, and his shame will never be wiped away."[9]

We watched the career of a minister go down in flames because of his tryst with a secretary. His church was devastated by the revelation. He repented by publicly acknowledging his sin. His wife stood by him. Then he fell again. And again. Finally, he was driven from the ministry permanently. His wife died prematurely. His daughter lost faith in life and God. Were the few minutes of excitement worth the price of a destroyed ministry, marriage, and child?

That's the reality of adultery. It isn't glamorous. It isn't fulfilling. It isn't a solution. Ask those who have had to live with the consequences of adultery, and if they're completely honest with you, most will admit it was the worst mistake of their lives.

It's said that when the smallpox virus reached the Hawaiian Islands it devastated the native population. It was a new disease against which the islanders had no natural immunities. While many died of the disease itself, many more needlessly died from pneumonia. When struck by the high fever of smallpox generates, they rushed into the cool waters of the Pacific to find relief and contracted pneumonia. A serious problem turned into a fatal one through a remedy more dangerous than the disease.

The same is true of adultery. Rushing into an affair to find relief from an unhappy marriage is a dangerous decision. The headaches of a bad marriage are mild compared to the migraine consequences of sexual infidelity.

LIVING WITH AN "ARRANGEMENT"

When Bob was a new pastor, we decided to visit some of the elderly members of our congregation, including a couple in their late eighties who had been married well over fifty years. From the moment we stepped into the living room, we could have cut the tension with a knife. The couple seated themselves at ninety-degree angles to each other, and rather than talk directly to each other, they asked me to mediate.

"Pastor, tell her to stop nagging me about my chores," the old man said.

"You can tell him I'm not nagging him. He just won't admit that he needs to slow down. Tell him he's a stubborn mule," she countered.

And so it went. When we finally left the house, we were relieved that at least no chairs had been tossed our way. We couldn't believe it. After fifty years they still weren't speaking to each other.

For unhappy couples who reject the idea of divorce, and would never consider having an affair, the third option is usually called an "arrangement." They agree to stay together, but to live separate lives. They share the same roof, but seldom the same bed. They have their names on the credit card account, but rarely on anniversary cards to each other. To the outside world they look like a happy household, but inside, the four walls of their home are papered with animosity and resentment.

I (Bob) once visited a couple in which the man was dying of cancer and had, at most, two months to live. Although he and his wife had always had a stormy marriage, I thought that perhaps now as the end was so close they would soften towards each other. But as I sat in the living room that day, trying to show concern and love for the dying man, she stormed in and berated him for forgetting to take his medicine. Their patterns were so deeply ingrained that they could not change, even in the face of death.

Living Alone Together

Few people choose to stay in unhappy marriages anymore. In our grandparents' generation, couples would admit they made a mistake getting married, but they would often negotiate an armed truce. It didn't create loving marriages or stable home environments for children, but it kept them from experiencing all the problems of divorce and adultery. People would sleep in different parts of the house, eat alone, and often go to church by themselves.

Today we basically see the same phenomenon in marriages where husbands and wives essentially lead separate lives. They keep separate checkbooks, work different schedules, and take vacations by themselves. The spouses merely share expenses and household duties and occasionally appear with each other in public. The marriage is primarily a business partnership.

We believe many couples who settle for an arrangement once genuinely loved each other. They got married believing they would intimately share their lives and end up in their seventies or eighties walking down the street hand in hand. They never foresaw the day when their lovemaking would be as exciting as vacuuming the carpet or reading spam emails. They never dreamed they would go for an entire week without eating a single evening meal together. Nor did they anticipate it would be more fun to spend a weekend with friends from the office than alone with each other.

What happened? They starved their relationship to death. Strong marriages take time. Willard Harley, a marriage therapist and author of *His Needs, Her Needs*, claims that a couple needs fifteen hours a week of uninterrupted time alone to maintain a healthy marriage.

But when you subtract the time spent commuting to work, putting in a full day at the office, working out at the gym, surfing the Net, attending meetings, and catching up on reading or the latest movies, today's couples have precious little time left to work on intimacy and communication. They may have achieved their career goals, hopped onto the corporate fast track, and bought the largest house in their subdivision, but it was at the expense of the one relationship intended to last a lifetime.

For example, couples who spend their leisure time in individual activities or with people other than their spouse are most likely to experience marital distress. You can't build a relationship if you aren't spending time together.[10]

Let us illustrate. I (Bob) have always been an amateur gardening enthusiast (I need to stress the word "amateur"). Once when we moved to a new community, we read in the paper that the village gardening club rented plots in the summer to residents. I jumped to the phone, called the president of the organization, and learned there were just two plots left. "I want them both," I proudly told

Cheryl. *Miracle Grow© is about to find itself another world champion,* I thought to myself. Even as I hung up, I imagined myself wheeling home bushels of plump tomatoes, ripe green peas, and succulent corn on the cob. Perhaps I would even have to cart the excess harvest to the local farmer's market on Thursday mornings.

When I went to inspect my two choice plots, I discovered they were so far at the other end of the field that they people rototilling their plots looked about three inches high. I also discovered my plots were an enormous distance from the nearest water spigot. I would need five hoses from the local fire brigade just to reach my garden. *No problem,* I thought, *it's bound to rain a good deal this summer.*

On June 16th, the day of our wedding anniversary, I dragged Cheryl to a local nursery to buy an assortment of seedlings and plants to jump-start my garden. For the next two hours we lovingly planted tomatoes, green beans, bell peppers, lima beans, corn, and a variety of leafy vegetables. I assured Cheryl that our efforts would be rewarded by lowering our veggie budget that summer. When I finally put the last shoot in the ground, I announced we could then go out and have our anniversary supper together.

Every now and then I would drive by our plots and nod my head in satisfaction. Even though I couldn't see my garden from the road—at least not without binoculars—I knew in my heart that champion greens were bursting through the earth at that very moment.

Days passed, and I found myself preoccupied at work. Our oldest son was in baseball, my wife was exhausted from caring for our three preschoolers, and we were trying to sell a car. So most nights by the time I got home and finished supper and helped put the kids to bed, I was too tired to drive to the plots.

But the rains came that summer as I had hoped. In fact, it rained and rained and rained. After several weeks of neglecting the plots I took my children with me to check on them. We weren't in the garden for more than two minutes. Mosquitoes the size of pigeons came swarming out of the grass and trees and chased us back to our car.

Then it was time for our three-week vacation. By our return home in August, I hadn't been to the plots for over a month. I suddenly remembered the ominous memo the garden club president had issued at the beginning of the summer, "Individuals who do not tend to their garden will not be granted privileges for the next year." Fearful of the garden's condition by now, I did the only natural thing a person does when dreading the truth—I avoided it.

By the end of August I could no longer put off the inevitable. Taking my trusted friend, John, with me for moral support, I drove to the garden. I knew it wouldn't be pretty, but a man has to do what a man has to do.

"Come with me. I'll show you my two plots," I said to my comrade. We walked forever past rows of huge watermelons, oversized squash, and towering corn. At last, we reached the stakes indicating my land.

"Where is it?" he asked innocently.

"Where's what?" I retorted.

"Your garden. Where is it? I don't see it anywhere."

I looked around. He was right. The garden had entirely disappeared underneath weeds as tall as mature oak trees. I got down on my knees and dug through the grass, looking for any sign of vegetable life. But the entire garden had just disappeared.

The weeks of neglect had taken their toll. My labor of love now looked more like a jungle than a vegetable plot. The closest I would come that summer to enjoying fresh vegetables was drinking a can of V-8 left in the bottom of the refrigerator.

Marriage is much like gardening. We can start off with high hopes and grandiose expectations, but as we are distracted by the pressures of daily living life in your marriage. We let the weeds begin to grow. Given enough time, they choke the life out of every healthy plant in the soil. Then comes the day, often too late, when we discover the enormity of our loss.

As we said earlier, we don't believe people set out to ruin their marriages. Few people return home from honeymooning in the Poconos or in St. Thomas intent on ignoring their partner for the rest of their lives. Newlyweds opening gifts at the reception aren't thinking, some day we'll show more courtesy to the UPS delivery man than to each other. But it happens.

Should you find your marriage in the same condition as my garden, do something. Don't let apathy and negligence choke out the last bit of life in your marriage. Don't settle for barren matrimony. Fight back. Regardless of how unfruitful the last several months or years have been, don't give in to the lie that love can't be renewed.

Rekindling the Flame

Within the character of God there is grace – the unearned, unmerited, freely given favor of God. When all seems hopeless and feelings of love toward our spouse are only a memory, the grace of God can do what we never thought possible. It can breathe life into a marriage that died years ago. It can restore tenderness to a relationship crusted over by years of apathy and neglect. It can revive a first love that has become last place in our life.

One of the most difficult interviews we ever conducted as writers was with a couple who has absorbed severe seismic shocks in their marriage. First, John and Nancy discovered their children had been molested by a teenager in their church. When they tried to expose the crime, the church refused to acknowledge it.

John's income wasn't meeting expenses, so he was forced to resign his job and look for work elsewhere. During this time, Nancy discovered she was pregnant—with twins. With little or no health insurance, they struggled to keep their heads above water financially. Soon after the birth of the twins, Nancy was diagnosed with cancer and underwent a hysterectomy.

Nancy and John just couldn't cope. The daily trauma cauterized their feelings. They went through the motions of marriage, but they became strangers to each other, bonded only by their mutual pain.

During this time John and Nancy moved and began seeing a counselor. Nancy happened on a book entitled *Rekindled* by Pat Williams, the former general manager of the Philadelphia 76er's basketball team. Williams wrote about his troubled marriage, which had nearly suffocated under the enormous pressures of his job. But he wanted his wife's love back, and he decided to fight for it.

When John read *Rekindled*, a spark was ignited in his own life. Despite the tragedy and suffering they had experienced, he was determined to win back his wife's love.

"The turning point came when John wrote a song and gave it to me," Nancy remembers. "I realized he was hurting as much as I was and that he still did cherish me."[10]

Marriage was never intended to be an arrangement of business associates. Marriage is meant to excite, stimulate, nurture, challenge, and encourage us for a lifetime. God's purpose is for it to provide us with intimate companionship, fulfilling partnership, and satisfying relationship. While the fire might not remain at the same level for a lifetime, the spark between two spouses need never die. Listen to the writer of Proverbs: "May your fountain be blessed, and may you rejoice in the wife of your youth. A loving doe, a graceful deer—may her breasts satisfy you always, may you ever be captivated by her love."[11] An "arrangement" might be one solution to a troubled marriage, but it is far from the best. Why settle for less than what God has planned for you?

COMMITMENT — THE RIGHT CHOICE

Divorce, adultery, and an arrangement—each offers temporary relief at best, and in the end each creates more problems and pain than it solves. There has to be a better way—and there is. But the only way out is through. We can't run from our problems. Believe me, if there were a better alternative available to couples than gutting out the problems with children, sex, financial pressures, in-laws, aging, taxes, and all the other tough issues in life, someone would have found it by now.

When I (Cheryl) was pregnant with all of our children, I suffered incredible nausea during the first trimester and part of the second trimester. If I even smelled coffee, I would double over right on the spot. It took nothing at all to make me throw up. I just threw up night and day. Over six pregnancies, I must have thrown up 2,000 times. Bob felt helpless. He would go to the grocery store a dozen times, searching for something he thought I might be able to keep down—all in vain.

I would continue to get worse, and finally the decision would be made to hospitalize me. As my health would deteriorate there were days when we wondered if either I or the baby would survive the ordeal (or if Bob would).

"Just wait," the doctors would assure us. "This will probably pass when you reach the second part of the second trimester." Terrific. That meant still more weeks of vomiting, going to the emergency room or hospital for intravenous feeding, and Bob watching me suffer.

How many days we both wished there were an easy way out of the nightmare. One night I had a reaction to the anti-nausea drug prescribed for me, and the muscles in my neck tightened so that I was partially paralyzed.

Bob at this point got very angry. He stalked through the house moaning, "I've had enough of this. I can't take it any longer. I'm sick and tired of living this way." (Of course I was the one with the actual problem. But Bob had just decided it was *his* turn to be seated at the head table of a pity party thrown in *his* honor.)

But we were committed. Committed to preserving the life of the baby and committed to seeing this thing through. Sure enough, just as month five began, a remarkable thing happened. Bob was eating a sandwich one day when I looked over at him and said, "I think I'd like a bite of that." In utter disbelief Bob handed me the sandwich and watched me take a few, tentative bites. Bob was overwhelmed. At last, at long last, I was able to eat again.

Four months later our first child was born. "It's a boy!" Bob yelled in the delivery room. Tears came from pure joy.

Commitment, sheer commitment aided by the grace of God saw us through those agonizing days. And because we stuck with it, we have a son (and five other children) who are the supreme joys of our life.

When marriage partners think they can't take another day and they want an easy way out, our counsel is to remember "The only way out is through." There is no question about it—commitment is the only solid foundation for a marriage. The Category Five hurricanes of life may tear off the roof over your head, blow out the windows around you, and leave you knee-deep in water, but when the storm is over, your relationship will survive.

No Love without Risk

Few generations in the history of our nation have been more fearful of commitment than this one. William Willimon, a cultural observer, quotes the author of *The Postponed Generation*: "Committed, lasting relationships are a critical aspect of maturity. Today's young adults are having more trouble with relationships than with almost any other area of their lives." As Willimon points out: "Adolescence just goes on and on. Just 'living together' keeps commitment in limbo. Somehow, these 'special children' reason, there has to be a way to find love without risk. So a *recent New York Times* article spoke of this as 'The Uncommitted Generation,' where sex and love are merely an experience in 'Being Alone—Together.'"

That's an excellent description of our generation: "Alone—Together." People who want love without risk never find it.

When Willimon was a part-time professor at Duke University, he once asked his students what they thought of the idea of living together outside of marriage as long as people are open, trusting, and caring. A young male student, barefooted and wearing a muscle shirt and blue jeans, was the first to speak up. "I've lived through three or four of these so-called relationships. I'm here to tell you there's no way for them to be open, trusting, and caring, no way in heck without a promise. I hurt some good people to find that out. I wish the church had told me. I might still have learned the hard way, but I wish the church had told me."[12]

What the young man was saying is also confirmed by studies that document the negative impact of living together before marriage. Such couples report both a lower quality of marriage and a greater likelihood of divorce than those couples who did not cohabit before the wedding. In fact, the longer a couple has lived together, the more pronounced the adverse impact on their later marriage. If living together before marriage is supposed to strengthen a relationship, just the opposite happens.[13]

A USA Today headline once announced: "Warning: Life Can Kill You." That's just the point. All of life requires a certain amount of risk. We can't leave our house in the morning, pull onto the freeway, or sit down at Starbuck's without exposing ourselves to some risk. We can't even use a credit card at a restaurant without fear of identity theft. Life itself is lethal. There simply is no way to play it safe.

Who Needs a Marriage License?

Ironically, those who avoid marriage and opt for "no commitment" relationships run the greatest risk of getting hurt. They set themselves up for a fall. Their unwillingness to commit virtually ensures they'll be taken advantage of.

Would we buy something on eBay if it offered no safeguards? Would we buy a car from a dealer who scoffed at warrantees as outmoded? Would we hand our credit card to a travel agent who thought issuing a receipt was for our parents' generation? We'd have to be crazy to do business with merchants who refused to make and honor a promise to their customers. Yet, when it comes to signing a wedding certificate or legalizing vow, the "no commitment" generation scoffs at marriage as archaic.

One of the saddest calls we have ever received was from a woman whose boyfriend just announced one morning he was leaving. "I can't handle our relationship any longer," he said. With that, he put his things in his car and drove off. The woman in tears asked if we could help bring him back. We were moved with pity and compassion, but there was nothing we could do. She had agreed to no commitment going into the relationship, and that's exactly what she got out of it.

There is absolutely no other foundation for happiness in human relationships than committed love. And that's part of growing up. As Willimon says so eloquently, "Welcome to reality. Life, you can be sure, has its grim side. Don't settle for anything less than a promise that will enable you to persevere in your love....We Christians know of no happiness save that which arises as the by-product of commitment to each other. We have no definition of love (a cross being on our altar) that is sacrifice—or risk-free. Relationships between men and women that go beyond merely hanging around take time, hard work, tough-mindedness, and a host of other virtues."[14]

Commitment begins with a promise. And if we keep our vows, they'll keep us. One hundred couples married forty-five years or more were asked to tell what factors had contributed most to keeping them together in stable and satisfying marriages for over four decades. Their answers? Marrying someone you enjoy being with, keeping a sense of humor, agreeing on your life's goals, and not surprisingly—a commitment to each other and marriage.[15]

That's why of all the options available to couples struggling with their relationship, commitment is still the right choice.

IF YOU KEEP YOUR VOWS, THEY'LL KEEP YOU

OVER THE YEARS we have sat through some truly strange, if not bizarre, wedding ceremonies. In place of the traditional lifelong, exclusive, binding commitments to each other, we have heard neutered, devalued, mass media vows taken from some Blog on the Internet:

> I, Meredith promise you, Brian, that I will always have your back. I'll text message you often, and when my schedule allows it, I'll meet you for Jamba Juice (I'll even pay for a "boost" in your Strawberries Wild.) I'll never cramp your style, spill my Chai-tea on your leather seats, or ask you to miss Sports Center. I know all these things so deeply define you as a person.
>
> In return, I ask that you honor my desire to drive a hybrid Hummer, to spend weekends with my sorority sisters, go over my minutes on my cell phone, and watch American Idol.

As the bridesmaids (or bridesmen) dab tears from their eyes, deep calls unto deep, and the groom responds with an equally profound pledge:

> I, Brian, take you, Meredith, to be my life partner. I will, from this day forward, give you full access to my DVD collection, Blackberry, iPod, and my Platinum Visa card. I'm offering you the chance to join me in a pursuit of who we really are, in sharing a room on a MySpace site, booting up together to face life. I shall never ask you to give up e-trading in the market or move your Bowflex out of the bedroom.
>
> In return, I ask that you let our 85-lb. black lab sleep in our room, let me eat Fruit Loops for dinner, and never complain about my selections for my Fantasy Football team.

As smooth jazz plays in the background, the couple turns around and heads down the aisle to begin their newfound joint partnership, which has been spelled out and ratified in a ten-page prenuptial agreement (copies available at the back of the church). The lawyers shake hands in the reception line, and the deal is done.

BLOGOSPHERE VOWS

The only problem with these downloaded vows is that they haven't promised anything resembling marriage. While they do touch on critical areas such as exercise regimens, stock portfolios, and ownership of hot cars, they never mention the more upsetting and unpleasant topics such as sickness, poverty, and the most unmentionable of all—death.

Today, wedding vows are seen more as flexible goals rather than as solemn words of honor to be kept to the death. How else can you explain the staggering divorce statistics of the last four decades and the high percentage of men and women who admit to cheating on their mate? They've obviously been able to rationalize away the promises they made in front of God, the state and their families.

And those people who are troubled by the idea of breaking a promise just don't make them, even when they get married. They rewrite the wedding ceremony and leave out the unpleasant parts—"for better or worse, richer or poorer, in sickness and in health." It's perhaps no coincidence that in the 1970's, the decade when divorce became all the rage, the popularity of writing your own wedding vows took off as well. If you didn't promise much, you hadn't broken much when you cut out.

ONLY A MATTER OF SEMANTICS?

Some have altered the traditional wording of the wedding vows to now read "for as long as we both shall love" instead of "for as long as we both shall live." The distinction between the two pledges is more than semantic; it's significant. The newer vows state that I'm only willing to stay married as long as I believe I'm in love. If I lose the feeling, if the tingle diminishes or the spark dies out, the relationship is so yesterday's news. One bad fight, one lousy weekend, or too many visits from the in-laws, and it's time to start a Google search for an attorney.

Notice the subtlety of the new emphasis. My pledge isn't based on what I choose, but what I feel. So if I no longer feel like I love my spouse, then I'm no longer obligated to keep my vows. I can cheat on my mate, trash my promise, and break up our home—all because my feelings have changed.

But if you read the traditional vows closely, you find they don't contain any escape clauses, except one—death. The only way a marriage was designed to end is at a funeral. That's the Creator's bottom line for commitment; it's for keeps.

The promises we made at our wedding ceremony are not only considered by the state to be legally binding, enforceable, permanent contract, but by God as well. He designed the idea of marriage. Imagine getting your photos back and discovering God standing in the middle of the wedding party. We suspect that would cause all of us to hesitate more before reneging on our vows.

As our society has devalued the integrity and permanence of wedding vows, we have dramatically decreased the chances of finding lasting fulfillment in marriage. The easier it is to get out, the easier it becomes to give up. The result is a culture of desperately hurting, lonely, and unhappy people who trade in spouses the way they trade in used Honda Civics.

It's our conviction that a promise isn't a promise until we keep it even when we no longer want to.

We quickly discovered how difficult life can be and how vows will be tested, even when you are in love. While we were still engaged, we put our names on a waiting list for married student housing. But when we returned to seminary as newlyweds in the fall, there were still no openings. So we set out to find an apartment off-campus that could become our own little love nest. As newlyweds all we wanted was a place to snuggle and study until graduation.

All we could find was a converted garage. (We came later to question the sincerity of its conversion experience.) If we were to try to entitle our first year in this dwelling, we would call it *Dark Night of the Garage* (not to be confused with *Dark Night of the Soul*, a classic written during the Middle Ages).

When we say converted garage, we mean exactly that. The landlord had decided to boost his retirement income by refinishing the basement area and making it into an apartment. He did all the plumbing and electrical work himself, which became quite apparent once we moved in.

To begin with, every time the landlord's wife would do laundry and the washer would hit the rinse cycle, the brownish gray water would come gushing into our kitchen sink. We would have only ten seconds to run from the table and grab dishes from the sink before they were engulfed in swirling muddy water. If we listened closely for the sound of her washer, we could usually anticipate the deluge and save ourselves from having to scald the dishes. When we complained about this minor inconvenience, she replied, "I don't see what you're so upset about. Our clothes aren't even dirty when we wash them."

Then winter arrived. And the cold winds began blowing. And the temperature dropped precipitously inside our apartment. For weeks we wore heavy sweaters, shivered under the covers day and night, and tried in vain to boost the temperature. The landlord and his wife were gone for several weeks— perhaps to a warmer climate—and could not be reached.

We were finally able to get one of their relatives to come and size-up our situation. He poked around and eventually stuck his hand into the heating duct that went to the main furnace—and pulled out several inches of pink fiberglass insulation. For whatever reason, the entire duct had been stuffed closed with insulation, seriously impairing the flow of heat to our apartment. (If it was an energy saving device, it worked.)

We managed to hang on until spring when the rainy season arrived. Much to our surprise, we discovered we had rented lake front property. Long before Jacuzzis were in vogue, we had water lapping at our feet inside the living room.

A few weeks before our lease was up our landlord decided to throw a dinner party on the patio directly above our apartment. Call it coincidence, call it passive aggressive bahvior, even call it petty revenge, but we decided this would be a good night to cook out. We loaded our little grill with charcoal and then poured on enough lighter fluid to fuel a 767 aircraft on a transatlantic flight. When we lit the match, smoke billowed up, and a favorable wind wafted it across the patio. The singing and laughter from upstairs inexplicably came to a stop.

As you can imagine, all these adversities challenged our young marriage. We don't remember the specifics, but we think we did discuss once or twice whose idea it was to sign the lease. But the ironclad marriage vows we had exchanged the year before helped get us through our *Dark Night of the Garage*. We had promised both God and man we would hang in there, even when threatened by freezing temperatures, sinks full of black-wash, and floodwaters that reached our sofa. We're glad we did.

Because we kept our vows, they kept us.

That's why we object so strongly to tinkering with marriage pledges. If we reword them to apply only as long as we feel love for the other person, a thousand

and one things can happen to turn our dream house into a heartbreak hotel. It's when we're under incredible stress that genuine wedding vows show their true genius and power. They will get you through the worst possible moments of your life. They will bond you in a way that no cheap substitute can duplicate or imitate. As the commercial says, "Don't settle for anything less."

THE ONLY WAY OUT IS THROUGH

But if our marriage isn't working, and divorce, adultery, or an armed truce isn't the way to go, what should we do?

The way to renew a marriage is not with a change of emotions, but with an act of the will. Renewal begins when we make the decisive choice to live up to the promises we have made. Even if we have broken them in the past, we can decide today never to do it again—and mean it. We can begin again where we first began—with vows that were meant "for keeps".

You may be thinking, "But you don't understand. My marriage is so bad. It's so empty. It's so unfulfilling. Why in the world should I commit myself to staying in this dead-end relationship?" Because no problem can be solved by running from it. Remember, the only way out is through. We can't assure you that your marriage will be transformed overnight if you choose to keep vows, but we can absolutely guarantee it will be ruined if you choose not to do so. The only hope toward restoring joy and fulfillment in our relationships is to live by the promises and pledges we made to our spouses. It's the design for marriages that work.

Perhaps the only thing going for your marriage at this point is determination not to give up. You're in good company. In the Bible there is a story in Genesis about a man who never let disappointment or temptation bring him down.

Joseph was traded away into slavery by his older brothers. He was then given a place of prominence in his master's house only to finally be thrown into prison. He did someone a favor to get him out of prison but the man promptly forgot him.

But eventually the man who was released from prison remembered that Joseph was a man who was correct in interpreting dreams. The paroled man eventually told Pharaoh that Joseph was a remarkable man who could correctly interrupt dreams.

Joseph was brought before Pharaoh. Joseph quickly told him what his dreams meant concerning a famine in the near future and how to plan for the upcoming disaster. Pharaoh was so impressed with Joseph he put him in charge of all the day to day operations in the land. Joseph who had never given up through many years was now second in the land only to Pharaoh himself:

> So Pharaoh said to Joseph, "I hereby put you in charge of the whole land of Egypt." Then Pharaoh took his signet ring from his finger and put it on Joseph's finger. He dressed him in robes of fine linen and put a gold chain around his neck. He had him ride in a chariot as his second-in-command, and men shouted before him, "Make way !" Thus he put him in charge of the whole land of Egypt.   Genesis 41:41-43

There is an enormous amount of hope in the story of Joseph. The difference between the marriage that crashes and burns and the one that reaches the half-century mark is this: One couple gives up; the other does not.

Ultimately the only way to fail in life or in marriage is to give up. If we keep getting up, coming back, and refusing to say "die," eventually we will prevail.

MOVING FROM "I DO" TO "I WILL"

Glamour magazine published an article entitled "The Five Turning Points of Love." The author, Lesley Dormen, suggested that the most crucial decision of a love relationship is the last one, when a couple is ready to create something bigger than both of them. She illustrates with the example of Karen and Joe:

"On my wedding day, I remember looking at Joe in a kind of horror thinking, Who is this stranger?" says thirty-two-year-old Karen. "I'd only known all the guests for decades. I'd known the groom for only a year and a half!" Three years into the marriage, when Karen was pregnant, Joe's business failed. "Our commitment was really on the line. This wasn't 'Will he remember our anniversary?' or 'Will he be angry because I was late to the theater?' The crisis marked the time both of us really felt, 'No matter what happens, we're in this together."[1]

The turning point of a marriage is in a moment of crisis when there is nothing to sustain the two of you but your promise to remain married for a lifetime. It's the point at which a marriage no longer rides on the promise "I do" but "I will."

The payoffs from deciding to stick with it begin almost immediately and are valuable beyond description. Dormen says, "As your commitment matures, intimacy grows steadily, then levels off. You begin to be less focused on your mate, more involved in creating something bigger than the two of you—a family, a home, a business, a spiritual life."[2]

But you'll never discover the "something bigger than the two of you" if you give up. The man or woman who cheats on a spouse has given up. The man or woman who files for divorce to advance a career has given up. Far too many couples give up far too soon and as a result miss the beauty and meaning their marriage could have.

CHOOSE TO LET YOUR MARRIAGE LIVE

It's like the despondent teenager who contemplates suicide because he has been rejected by the college he wants to attend. A loving and mature adult would put his arm around such a hurting person and say, "Don't do it. There's still so much life ahead. You can't even begin to imagine all the wonderful experiences awaiting you in your twenties and thirties and beyond. As bad as this is, don't take away the possibility of experiencing marriage, parenthood, and a career. I know your heart has been broken, but it will heal. There are other schools and other careers that are worthwhile. Life is still ahead of you."

Yet, when marriages are still in their adolescence, and major disappointments enter the picture, couples assume the only solution is to turn out the lights on the relationship. Our advice is, "Don't do it. We know the pain and disappointment are bad right now, but don't kill this relationship. That's not the answer. Your life together is still ahead of you."

Like the teenager who chooses to live, couples need to make similar commitment to let their marriages live. And the place to begin is by making a mutual commitment to keep your vows, even if you don't feel like doing so at the moment.

This advice doesn't apply just to couples on the verge of splitting up, but also to couples with relatively stable marriages who feel their relationship has grown stale. We issue the same challenge. Go back to your vows. Consider again exactly what you promised to each other. Then take the difficult but monumental step of saying, "I'm going to keep my word. I'm going to keep the promise I made on my wedding day. I'm not going to quit."

REFRESHING YOUR MEMORY

Let's assume you accept the idea "If you keep your vows, they will keep you." Let's also assume that in the wedding ceremony you went beyond pledging to share your iPod and recited more traditional vows. What did you agree to?

"Will you take this person to be your wedding spouse, to live with according to God's law in the holy state of matrimony? Will you love, comfort, honor and keep (him/her), in sickness and in health? And, forsaking all others, will you keep yourself only unto (him/her), so long as you both shall live?"

If we can get past the Elizabethan English, what we discover is that the two of you agreed to something rather remarkable. In fact, it's one of the most profound, incredible, and wondrous contracts two people ever enter into in this life. To what have you signed on in this binding contract?

I Chose of My Own Free Will to Marry This Person

You were asked by the minister if you wanted "to take this person to be your wedded spouse." All you had to say was "No thanks," and the whole thing would have ended right there. But no, you said, "I do."

It's a sign of both maturity and character to live up to the choices we make. Watch little children at an ice cream counter trying to choose from thirty-one flavors. They pace the floor, their little noses pressed against the glass to get a closer look, the "I need to make this count" expression on their face. After much agonizing, the choice is finally made. Inevitably, one of the children will say, "Oh no. I wish I had gotten what you got." The child then sits down, face downcast, and reluctantly eats his ice cream cone, consumed with remorse that he didn't order blue moon instead of peanut butter crunch.

Married couples often do the same thing. They make a free and uncoerced choice to marry one person and then spend the rest of their lives lamenting the fact they didn't marry someone else. They miss the one opportunity given to them for happiness because they won't accept the responsibility of their own choice.

We promised our mates that we were making this choice of our own free will. We said we were doing it in all sincerity and truth. We need to reaffirm that choice. We need to quit window-shopping, looking in the rearview mirror, or staring in envy at someone else's husband or wife, and accept the gift we have been given.

Brianna, who came from a troubled home, had serious trouble making commitments. She would swing back and forth from wanting to work out her problems with her husband to deciding to remove all her things from the house at night. We tried to help her see it was her choice to marry Philip and that for her own personal stability and character she needed to stay with that choice.

She said she would. Then she changed her mind. Then she changed it back. Ultimately she divorced her husband, and soon after the decree was granted, married another man.

You chose your mate of your own free will. The secret of contentment is to celebrate that choice, to treat it with honor, and to put out of your mind forever the idea you'd be happier with someone else. Why? Because you promised you would. And, if you continue to second-guess yourself, you will blow the only real chance you have to find joy and satisfaction in your marriage.

I Choose to Live According to God's Law of Love

We promised "to live with (our spouse) according to God's law in the holy state of matrimony." Our belief about the number one problem in most troubled marriages might surprise you. It isn't sex. It isn't money. It isn't the in-laws. It's that couples have left God out of their relationship.

Alexander Solzhenitsyn, the famous Russian author and historian, was forced from his native land in the 1970s and immigrated to the United States. His address to the graduating class of Harvard is regarded by many as one of the most significant addresses of the 20th century. He told the graduates that day that the entire history of that century, with all its wars and famines and revolutions, could be summarized in one simple statement: "Men have forgotten God." The press ridiculed him, and the intellectual community at Harvard scoffed at his remarks, but he was absolutely right.

Marriage is simply a microcosm of human relationships. Just as nations suffer pain and upheaval when they forget God, so do men and women who try to live together without God.

Jesus said, "Haven't you read...that at the beginning the Creator 'made them male and female,' and said, 'For this reason a man will leave his father and mother and be united to his wife and the two will become one flesh'? So they are no longer two, but one. Therefore what God has joined together, let man not separate."[3] Did you notice that last point? What God has "joined together."

Although Bob has officiated at numerous weddings, he has never married anyone. God does that; he simply acts as his representative. We have no power to take two separate humans and, by reciting a ritual, turn them into "one flesh." Only God has that transformational ability.

That precise point was driven home to a couple we know when they learned after the honeymoon that their wedding license was invalid. The minister who had performed the ceremony had flown in from out of state and had failed to register with the county. So the couple had to go through a second ceremony in order to have the license granted. The entire time they were on their honeymoon they weren't legally married (through no fault of their own). Although there was a glitch in the legal system, in the eyes of the Almighty they had done all they could do to become husband and wife. God is the one who joined them together the day they exchanged vows.

If it is God who joins people together, if he is the Creator who designed a couple's sexuality and attraction to each other, if he is the Master Architect of human relationships, how can two humans assume their relationship is comprised of just themselves. "Just you and me, baby...," the old love song goes. That's where trouble so often begins. Couples choose every other basis imaginable for their marriage except the one valid foundation—a biblical one.

We read with interest the story of a woman who wrote to a woman's magazine saying, "I still love my ex-husband." The couple had opened a kitchen supply store after they were married, and they had spent so much time on their business that the relationship deteriorated. One day the husband announced he had found someone else and was leaving. But the business demanded that the couple continue to work together throughout the divorce proceedings and even after he had remarried.[4]

This story is a tragedy. They built their marriage around business, not God. Even though the husband divorced his wife, married another, and was soon to be a father, the first wife still loved him. She did so because God had joined them together, and they were one flesh. You can't tear apart one flesh without inflicting deep wounds. Even then, the longing is to be whole again. This woman wasn't neurotic or unbalanced because she still loved and yearned for her husband. What she was feeling was the natural result of marriage.

When we lived in the Southwest, we met a couple who had purchased a home in a new subdivision out in the desert. It had everything they had ever wanted: spacious rooms, stylish exterior, lovely landscaping.

They woke up one day to find their pictures hanging at an angle. Soon they noticed the windows wouldn't shut tight. Finally cracks began snaking up the living room walls. They called the contractor in a tizzy. Their dream home was falling apart by the hour.

It turned out that their house had been built on a "wash," a dry riverbed that floods only during the rainy season, but the ground can be unstable. Every home in the subdivision experienced the same problems. The contractor eventually filed bankruptcy, and dozens of families were forced to abandon their homes because the foundations were inadequate to support the weight of the structures.

Couples who forget their pledge to "live according to God's law in the holy state of matrimony" are building their homes in a desert wash. Does that mean they'll divorce? Not necessarily. Does it mean they'll never be happy? No, they may work out a good relationship. But they will never know the full meaning and beauty of marriage unless they base it on having God as Lord and Master of their relationship. They are also taking tremendous risks that it will fail.

What is God's law for marriage? Jesus defined it in surprisingly simple terms: "'Love the Lord your God with all your heart and with all your soul and with all your mind.' This is the first and greatest commandment. And the second is like it: 'Love your neighbor as yourself.'"[5]

God's law for marriage is to love him first and foremost and then to love each other as much as we love ourselves. What is love? "Love is patient, love is kind. It does not envy, it does not boast, it is not proud. It is not rude, it is not self-seeking, it is not easily angered, it keeps no record of wrongs. Love does not delight in evil but rejoices with the truth. It always protects, always trusts, always hopes, always perseveres."[6]

Whenever I (Bob) look at this list, I think, "Whoa. I'm supposed to do all that? I wake up so grouchy when I don't get seven full hours of sleep that I need to be put into a containment tank till 9:00 a.m. Yet I'm supposed to be patient, kind, and nonenvious every day of my life? I don't think so."

That's precisely the point. We can't love another individual in the truest sense of the word unless we are in a relationship with God. He gives us the ability to override our selfish, cranky, and stubborn personality when we allow his love to flow through our lives.

We've seen that type of love lived out in marriages. Hal and Jeanette had been married for nearly forty years. For most of her adult life, Jeanette had lived with chronic rheumatoid arthritis. She had virtually every socket and joint in her body replaced with aluminum or plastic to ease her pain. She did not have an hour free of pain in two decades.

Her husband stayed with her through all those years. He literally had to lift her up from her chair and help her sit down. She could go nowhere without him. For years he did all the cooking, cleaning, and grocery shopping. He logged more hours in waiting rooms while surgeons worked on her frail body than he can remember. But we never heard him complain. Come to think of it, we never heard her complain either. Today she is free of all pain—in heaven.

What kept them together all those painful years? The love described by the apostle Paul. Early in their lives they dedicated their marriage to the Creator, and they remained loving and faithful to one another because of the love and faithfulness of God's character.

Wedding vows that fail to include promises to live according to God's design for marriage aren't complete. They may be good intentions, but chances are they won't be adequate to face problems such as Hal and Jeanette have faced and conquered.

I Choose to Treat My Spouse as a Person of Value

"Will you love (him/her), comfort (him/her), honor and keep (him/her), in sickness and in health?" That question cuts to the core issue of how we will view the person we're committing to spend the rest of our life with.

The story is told of a clever burglar who once entered a department store after hours. His goal was not to steal the merchandise but to create chaos by switching the price tags on scores of items. Fine French perfume was now marked at $1.95, while men's socks sold for $435.00. Leather shoes were a bargain at $.59 while umbrellas would set you back $265.00 plus tax. It was days before the store could reopen, because every item had to be checked to make sure it was marked with its proper value.

One way to disrupt or even destroy a marriage is to fail to treat our mates according to their value. When we belittle, criticize, ignore, neglect, or demean our husband or wife, we take fine French perfume and sell it for the price of a pair of men's socks. When respect goes, love soon exits as well.

We're surprised how many couples can't understand why they are so unhappy. They spend hours pointing out the faults of their mates, dwelling on their imperfections, and acting as if they were the biggest nuisance of their life, and yet can't understand why the feelings of love just aren't there anymore.

It's because they no longer value the person they are living with. Our minds and hearts listen to what we say and the way we treat our mates, and they respond accordingly. If we love, comfort, and honor another person in our everyday actions, our emotions are going to keep pace.

We'd like to challenge every husband and wife who think they have lost their feelings of love to try the following experiment. For three days treat your mates as if they are of enormous value to you. Go out of your way to show true respect, to listen with real intensity and without interrupting, and to compliment sincerely their strong traits. Keep your critical thoughts to yourself, and, instead, showcase their strengths to your friends and family. Anticipate their needs and put them first. Show affection even when it isn't for the purpose of making love. And give your mates time to relax and find solitude.

We will wager that after three days of acting this way your feelings will undergo a transformation. It's called cognitive dissonance. Our mind won't allow our feelings to exist contrary to our behavior. If we treat someone with love, honor, and respect, we are going to begin feeling it.

I (Bob) once spent a month with an Irish minister and his wife who were in their late sixties. While he was the guest speaker at our church for four weeks, I was to chauffeur him and his wife around the city. Those four weeks transformed my understanding of marriage.

The love affair that these two had sustained was extraordinary. Wherever they went, he treated her with dignity and respect. While chauffeuring them, I would listen to them talk to one another. Every two or three miles he would ask, "How are you, darling?" "Just fine," she would reply. He was just checking.

I contrast that to a scene my sister witnessed in a store where she worked. The manager's wife came in and showed her husband a new blouse she wanted to buy. "Why would you buy that?" he said so loud others could hear. "You know you're built like a man." Not surprisingly, they later divorced.

At no time is that attitude of value and respect more difficult to maintain than when a spouse's health fails. A mate's needs can become overwhelming, and the daily demands a burden. When the couple is no longer able to function in a typical marital relationship, the commitment to value each other is put to the supreme test.

We know two families who were hit hard by Alzheimer's disease. In the first case the wife was afflicted with the disease and eventually had to become institutionalized. When the medical costs began mounting, the husband filed for divorce to protect his assets. He was relieved of his burden to pay for her costs, and the state was forced to pick up the tab. Whatever his motives were, his wife died a divorced woman. It may have made sense economically, but we wonder how he rationalized way his promise to "love, comfort, honor, and keep her in sickness and in health."

Was he biblically correct in divorcing her? No. We believe the vow to value our spouses until the day they die is worth sacrificing everything we have, even if it costs every penny. Marriage is much more than protecting a pension or guarding our IRAs; it's valuing a human being above every other thing on earth. And as the Scripture says, where your treasure is, your heart is also.

The second couple responded quite differently. When it became apparent he was suffering from the dreaded disease, his wife, Maggie, said, "We have had a wonderful marriage for all these years. I could not have asked for a better husband. It is now my privilege to care for him. I know if the roles were reversed, Ross would do the same for me." She stayed faithful to the very end.

What's the difference between the two marriages? One sees their vows as situational pledges, the other as inviolable promises. When you marry, no one can promise that you'll retire rich, healthy, or whole. Your marriage may involve sacrifices that are unimaginable. But the pledge to value the other person, come what may, is what gives a couple the security and confidence to face the future.

I Agree to Be a Faithful Partner until the Day I Die

"And, forsaking all others, will you keep yourself only unto (him/her), so long as you both shall live." Do you remember saying that?

A radio and television talk show host once asked his audience, "If I were to give you a million dollars, would you agree to let me spend one night with your wife?" Callers were urged to dial a 900 number to register their vote. People who were interviewed on the street gave mixed reactions. It was clear that for price a surprising number of people would willingly compromise the sexual integrity of their marriage for a million bucks.

But as the talk show host later said, "The right answer is no. Regardless of how you rationalize it, entering into an agreement like that would forever change your marriage. It could never be the same."

He's right. Maintaining sexual integrity and purity in marriage gives it strength and meaning. There is one part of our life together that absolutely no one else on earth has the right to share. It is ours, and ours alone.

Frank Pittman, the author of *Private Lies: Infidelity and the Betrayal of Intimacy*, lists several popular fallacies about adultery that appear in cable television shows, supermarket tabloids, and even somepopular books on marriage.

Fallacy #1: Most people have affairs. As Pittman points out, surveys indicate the majority of married people stay true to their spouses. (An article in the *Chicago Sun Times* suggested the rate of infidelity between couples may be as low as 15 percent.)

Fallacy #2: An affair can be good for a marriage and can even revive a dull one. "Wrong," says Pittman. "The truth is most affairs do great damage. Overall, 53 of the 100 adulterous marriages I surveyed ended in divorce. This, in spite of the couples' decision to seek counseling and my own best effort to help them. By contrast, it is unusual in my practice for nonadulterous marriages to dissolve."

Fallacy #3: The lover is sexier than the spouse. "In my experience, lovers are not necessarily younger or more attractive than the spouse; nor is the affair necessarily about sex. Thirty of the people I surveyed—half men and half women—acknowledged that their sex lives at home were perfectly adequate. It was not sex but lack of intimacy that compelled them to have an affair.'"

The author summarizes his research by saying, "If there is one conclusion I can draw, it's that monogamy works. It isn't rare—it's practiced by most people most of the time, and always has been. It isn't difficult—anyone can do it, and only the smallest sacrifices are involved. Monogamy isn't even dull—living without lies and secrets opens you up to being known and understood, and that isn't dull."[8]

Yet the media sends us false messages. Several years ago I wrote a short piece entitled, "What If Beer Commercials Laster Longer than Sixty Seconds?" which deals with the fantasy that men are presented every time they watch football on Sunday afternoon. If they will just buy this particular brand of beer (or cologne, car, jeans, socks, toothbrush, topsoil, etc.), they can enjoy sexual relationships that defy description without cost or responsibility:

> The typical beer commercial features young, virile, and noticeably single men in their twenties and thirties. With the simple pop of a lid from a Coors Light, these males are able to command the appearance of their own private harem of young, exotic, and noticeably single nymphs.
>
> No courtship, no commitment, and no responsibility is required to enter this sexual Nirvana. No, just for the cost of a six-pack, any man can live out his most exquisite fantasy and never have to mow the lawn.
>
> In this sixty-second male-paradise, women exist only to satisfy the male thirst for hops and bed-hopping. In this best of all worlds, women satisfy libidos without demanding love, they surrender their

bodies without exacting promises, and they disappear from the screen without asking for alimony. Miraculously, there is never a morning after.

The commercials are as important for what they don't include as what they do. For example, there are never, I repeat never, wives, children, or heaven forbid, infants featured in the ads. They would clearly spoil the fun, and instantly pop the fantasy.

The message is clear. Pleasure and parenthood don't go hand in hand. The good life is one free of kids, commitment, and crab grass. The daily drudgeries of going to work, changing oil in the car, and painting the house are for the poor people who haven't discovered a Friday night poker game with Miller Genuine Draft. So order another cold one, bring on the babes, and forget phone bills, teenagers, and nagging wives.

But how does the Coors Light fantasy square with reality? Let's say the commercial runs longer than its appointed sixty seconds. The young, virile, and macho American male and the barroom babe fall in love. Their overpowering physical attraction, fueled by the high octane of a brewski, cannot be denied. Their passion reaches critical mass. He the great stud, and she the mystical nymph, must have one another.

After weeks of ecstasy, they move in together, then eventually marry. Fast-forward the tape a decade or so, and we discover that a tragic— and unforgivable—thing has happended in the land of the High Life.

She, like all of humanity, has started to get older. She no longer looks twenty, because she's now thirty. Worse yet, she's had a baby in the meantime. Its toll on her body is unacceptable. Besides stretch marks, her once Venus-like legs now have traces of varicose veins. She no longer fits in the bakini she wore on the mystical tropical island in her man's Budweiser fantasy.

"Hey, wait a second, this wasn't supposed to happen," thinks the stud. "Life is young chicks, good buddies who like to drink a lot, and blizzards that appear in the desert. It's not colic, garbage day, and wrinkles. I'm outta here," he says. "I deserve better. It would be wrong to deprive them of my rugged good looks and tough guy mystique. Macho men don't get older, they only get better." But the truth is our Genuine Draft dude is now developing problems of his own. He suffers from a Pabst Blue Ribbon tumor. His belly hangs sadly over the waist, resembling a giant lump of bread dough falling off a counter. His eyes also appear bloodshot. The top of his head glistens in the sun, evidence of a thinning plant life.

Our once invincible Adonis is growing older himself. But graying hair and good times don't go together. He knows better. So to deny the reality of the aging process, our macho friend heads back to the bar. Perhaps, over the next two decades, he repeats this cycle two or three times before he realizes what a fool he's been.

But it's too late. He long ago abandoned his wife to chase a fantasy that could only last sixty seconds. He gave up the love, power, and meaning of a lifetime commitment to live a fantasy no one actually lives.

His kids are grown and gone, and they want nothing to do with him. His "ex" is remarried and moved out of the state. All he's left with is a six pack. And as he puts yet another Bud Light to his lips, he realizes just how cold a cold one can be.[9]

The pledge to remain sexually faithful to another person is in your own best interest. It is the only possible arrangement that can offer a lifelong, fulfilling sexual relationship. Everything else has been tried, and it doesn't work.

Whoever owns the copyright to the initial version of the wedding vows had deep insight into human nature. "So long as you both shall live" is the only promise that makes marriage truly marriage. It's the only pledge that guarantees that both of you are truly serious about this union. Anything less than the promise of lifelong commitment is more like just going steady.

A sign outside of a Catholic monastery captured this truth: "You only go around once in life, but if done right, once is enough." You don't need a variety of partners, lovers, or spouses to experience the best life has to offer. It can be done with just one person. In fact, to truly experience life's best, it needs to be with just one person, for keeps.

That permanence gives our children security. It allows us to plan for our future once the children grow up and leave. It offers economic stability to our lives. It gives us a chance to form lasting friendships with others. It allows us to develop family traditions and create memories. The assurance that we will be together for as long as we live allows us to receive all the best things from life.

The wisest king ever to rule also acted perhaps the most foolishly. Solomon of ancient Israel took for himself over a thousand wives, believing that such vast numbers of lovers would offer him the ultimate satisfaction. Listen to his sad conclusion, "I denied myself nothing my eyes desired; I refused my heart no pleasure....Yet...everything was meaningless, a chasing after the wind; nothing was gained under the sun."[10]

CONCLUSION

Why should we keep our vows? Because they will keep us from wasting our lives, from squandering the sweetest gifts life can offer, and from coming down to our final days and saying, "It was all so meaningless." God has a better plan for you and me than that sad ending. But we can only discover it if we're willing to keep our promises.

When Bob's father returned home from World War II as a decorated air force pilot, his first words to Bob's mother were, "I promised you I'd come home." If you've been struggling with your marriage, let us offer you some good news. Your promises, if kept faithfully, will bring you home, too.

PART
TWO

PART
TWO

Chapter Five

REPAIRING YOUR MARRIAGE

SEAN AND KATIE STOOD IN THE BACKYARD of Sean's brother and carefully recited their vows. Many of the by-standers fought back tears—including their own three children. After twelve years of being divorced they were getting remarried and a family was being reunited.

What miraculous series of events led to this incredible moment of reconciliation? Only one, really...they had both chosen to forgive each other. The years of pain, betrayal, acrimony, brokenness, and alienation melted away under the healing warmth and light of God's gift to hurting relationships—*genuine forgiveness.*

How does a couple achieve not only forgiveness, but reconciliation as well? Let's look at the steps each couple must take to repair their marriage.

There must be sincere repentence.

We have several mistaken ideas about repentance in our culture. It is not simply saying, "I'm sorry." The fact that someone says he regrets holding up a bank is no indication he won't put on a ski mask and head for another savings and loan his first day out of jail. *Sorry* simply means he wishes he didn't have to face the consequences of his actions.

Nor is repentance acting depressed about our actions. There are rows of glum inmates in state prisons and county jails, but statistics tells us as many as 50 percent of them will be back there again some day. An emotional mood or state of mind doesn't prove a change of heart.

If saying "I'm sorry" isn't enough, if acting sad isn't adequate, and even if doing nice things doesn't erase the past, how do we show genuine repentance? For the answer we have to turn to the Scriptures. The New Testament word for *repentance* means "to undergo a change in frame of mind and feeling, to make a change of principle and practice, to reform by turning away from one's sins."

Genuine repentance in the case of adultery or pornography requires the offending spouse to undergo a radical change of practice and perspective. He or she cannot afford excuses such as "You weren't meeting my needs," "I was bored and needed some fun," or "It was only a one-time thing." The person needs to come to the point of saying, "What I did was inexcusable. It was selfish. It was foolish. It was egocentric. All I cared about was my own self-centered desires. I violated the most basic promise of our relationship for no good reason whatsoever." When someone reaches that point the process of genuine repentance has begun.

Genuine repentance never seeks to justify wrong actions; rather it owns the selfishness, the true sinfulness, the real pain the behavior has caused others. Don't settle for anything less than a genuine change in the frame of mind and feelings.

Genuine repentance also involves a change of outlook on the world. For example, people who repent of adultery now recognize that meeting their own needs, desires, and fantasies is not what marriage is all about. They re-orient their entire world-view from a self-centered one to a God-centered and spouse-centered perspective. They now realize that all the little lies, all the sneaking around, and all the irresponsible sexual encounters were symptoms of a diseased, sinful philosophy of life.

The final element of genuine repentance is a change of behavior. Spouses who have repented of infidelity no longer let their eyes wander at the office. They don't spend time teasing and flirting with others. They certainly don't call or arrange to meet their former lovers again for lunch. In fact, they don't meet any women for lunch.

Instead, they plan time alone with their spouse. When they find temptation tugging, they pick up the phone and call their husband or wife. They practice learning their spouses' needs, such as affection or companionship, and plan creative ways to meet them. They throw away any gift, token, or item that emotionally links them to their past affairs.

In other words, they actually start living differently. Until this type of genuine repentance is obvious, I would be cautious about believing a person has changed. While no one could accomplish all these thing overnight, the sense of progress must be there.

There must be a slow process of rebuilding trust
During the height of the Cold War in the 1980's, when leaders in the Soviet

Union were trying to negotiate a reduction in nuclear arms wth the United States, President Reagan often quoted a Russian proverb: "Trust, but verify."

On one occasion he stood next to General Secretary Gorbachev, then leader of the Soviet Union, and quoted this proverb. The Russian leader got visibly upset and interrupted him. "Why do you always say that?"

Always the gentleman, President Reagan smiled at him and politely replied, "Because it's true."

That same proverb will equally serve married couples who are recovering from past pain and disappointments. "Trust, but verify."

Even though a spouse appears to have undergone genuine repentance, he or she must undergo the painstaking process of earning back trust. Acts such as adultery, pornography, physical and emotional abuse, and emotional abandonment are serious offenses when it comes to trust. It is fraud, deceit, and betrayal at the deepest levels of a relationship.

So how does a couple rebuild trust? It begins with accountability. In the case of adultery, Dr. Willard Harley suggests the offending spouse draw up a daily time log, broken into fifteen-minute increments. The husband or wife who strayed fills in where he or she will be each of those fifteen minute segments of the day, complete with phone numbers. The other spouse is then given the prerogative to call or drop in at any time of the day, as often as desired.

Such cautious rebuilding makes sense. To immediately give back the keys to the bank to an employee who embezzled $250,000 would be an act of foolishness, not love and generosity. In the same way, to place trust in a husband or wife without requiring that partner to prove faithful over time is unwise.

There must be an understanding of the cost of forgiveness

I once heard a shock talk show host on a Chicago radio station pose the question to listeners, "If your spouse committed adultery, could you forgive and forget it happened?" Most of the callers responded, "I could probably forgive him [or her], but I doubt I could ever forget it." "Then you can't forgive them!" he would shout back. "Unless you forget, you haven't forgiven."

He was badly mistaken. Forgiveness doesn't imply we hypnotize ourselves or delete large sections of our lives from our memory banks. That's unrealistic, if not impossible. Forgiveness if not forgetting that something painful was done to us; it's releasing the other person from the moral debt he or she owes us.

Too often we trivialize forgiveness. Someone hurts us, apologizes, and we respond by saying, "No big deal." Minimizing what the other person did is not forgiveness. That's denial. Rather, forgiveness is making the costly decision to bear the injustice without requiring the other person to remain in our moral debt.

If people choose to forgive their spouses, they are taking on themselves the consequences of their mates' behavior without requiring payment for it. That's costly. That's difficult. That's the nature of forgiveness. That's exactly what Jesus Christ did for us on the cross: "He himself bore our sins in his body on the tree, so that we might die to sins and live for righteousness; by his wounds you have been healed" (I Peter 2:24).

Several years ago a man who had been a frequent speaker, a successful author, and a role model committed adultery. Yet, throughout the humiliation and pain of the ordeal, his wife chose to forgive him. She appeared in public by his side. She faced the people he had disappointed by his side. She even went on radio with him as he confessed his mistakes. It was an extremely difficult thing to do. It was his sin, not hers, but she acted as if it were hers as well. She was willing to bear the consequences of what he had done to her and others. Their marriage survived, and a new example of grace was given to the world.

DEVELOPING THE RIGHT ATTITUDES

Besides going through the right steps of forginving the past behaviors, it's also important that a couple develop the right attitudes toward each other. That calls for disposing of unproductive ideas and focusing on the positive convictions that make bonding possible.

Perhaps the most useless and counterproductive attitude for a spouse is, "I married the wrong person." As long as we think that, our marriage is going nowhere. As long as we believe we missed Mr. Perfect or Miss Ideal and married Mr. or Miss Second Best instead, we will feel miserable, angry, and trapped.

We can imagine someone saying, "But I did marry the wrong person. My mate is lazy, selfish, inconsiderate, dull, unattractive, hot-tempered, and eats too much!" Your description of your partner's character flaws and appearance may be absolutely right on all counts. But you still have to give up the idea that you married the wrong person, because as long as you insist your mate isn't right for you, he or she never will be.

The Power of a Changed Perspective

Think about it. What good does it do to label your spouse as "the wrong person"? Will it change him or her? Will it give either of you the desire and energy to work on your marriage? Will it bring out the best in your mate?

Dwelling on the belief you married the wrong person sets up a hopeless situation. If your mate is wrong for you, then it's a mistake to stay together. That opens the door to divorce and infidelity.

Instead, do something radical. Today, this very hour, give up for once and for all the idea you married the wrong person. Period. Permanently delete that data from your emotional computer, because it's the only way you can get back on track as a couple.

The power of a changed perspective can hardly be overstated. Bob Wieland is a war veteran who lost both legs in a land mine explosion. As Bob charged across an open field to pick up a wounded comrade, he stepped on a land mine designed to disable a multiton armored tank.

Bob had ample reason to feel sorry for himself. Prior to being drafted, he was an all-star college baseball player destined for the major leagues. The moment he stepped on the land mine he went from being over six feet tall to thirty six inches tall. His career in baseball was finished—forever.

But Bob had one thing going in his favor. He refused to give in to despair. He refused to believe his dream of being a professional athlete was over. And just a few years after his wounds, he won the world weightlifting title in the bench press. With only half a body, he lifted over three hundred pounds.

However, more setbacks were ahead. In an incredible decision, the judges later stripped of his title because of a technicality. What had he done wrong? He wasn't wearing shoes the day he won the world title.

But Bob is a man who refuses to give up. Instead of giving in to self-pity, he set out on a remarkable venture. He decided he would become the first man to crawl on his hands across the United States. It took him three years and eight months, but Bib Wieland pulled himself from the Pacific Ocean to the Atlantic, one hand at a time.

We share Bob's story because people caught up in the idea that they've married the wrong person can so easily lose perspective. Their anger, self-pity, and bitterness can blind them to the possibilities that still exist in their marriage.

Describe Your Spouse As His or Her Best Friend Would

Often our handicap is our negative attitudes. We challenge you to momentarily stop the tape inside your head that constantly repeats, "I married the wrong person," and, instead, write down all the positive things your spouse's best friend would say about him or her. What different spin would the friend put on the traits that irritate you? What you describe as boring, the friend might call stable. What you say is stinginess, another might compliment as frugality. What you label as obnoxious, someone else might call being the life of the party.

The truth is, in the beginning you probably were your spouse's best friend and saw his or her personality in the same positive light. It's time to go back and look at your spouse with fresh eyes. When you look again at your husband or wife respect and esteem, the positive characteristics will again emerge.

Drop the Excuses

Many people actually find their identity in suffering. They have grown so accustomed to feeling sorry for themselves and using excuses for not investing in their marriage that the idea of giving up those excuses is absolutely terrifying. Strange as it sounds, people may actually find comfort in the idea they have a horrible spouse. It gives them someone to criticize and keeps the attention deflected from their own shortcomings. It conveniently excuses their own lack of love and unselfishness and offers an escape route from the hard work of building a marriage.

Jana went through life telling her friends, "You know, people warned me that I should never marry Samuel. I wish I had listened to them." Apparently it never dawned on Jana that she was no real treat to live with either. In fact, of the two, Samuel was far more psychologically and emotionally healthy. But Jana's beliefs kept her from having to face the truth that she was deeply scarred, emotionally immature, and selfish.

Dropping our excuses can be frightening. What will I find if I face reality? What if I'm the failure? What if no one truly does love me? Those are legitimate fears. But again the reality is, there is no love without risk. If you are going to experience true love and intimacy in marriage, you're going to have to risk being vulnerable.

Many inmates fear parole more than prison. They know what it's like to live in a confined cell, to follow a prescribed regimen, and to have someone else order their lives for them day after day. But the idea of hitting the streets, finding a job, and adjusting to society can be terrifying. That is partially why so many convicts return to the penitentiary just a few years after release. We also can be so scarred of true intimacy and bonding that we won't give up the idea we married the wrong person. But that's where faith and risk taking make the difference between existing and living, cohabiting and becoming one flesh.

The Courage to Back over the Cliff

I (Bob) remember a time I was forced to face a persistent fear. I was working on staff at the church I grew up in, an inner city church that runs an aggressive summer program for kids. That summer we decided to go mountain climbing.

I have no idea why I agreed to go on this apparently suicidal venture to the Rocky Mountains. When we reached the remote base camp high in the mountains, I looked up at the gray, jutting peaks of the Sangre de Cristo mountains—and gulped.

We spent the first day in camp acclimating to the high altitude air. No problem. The second day we spent playing search and rescue. Great fun. The third day we put on belts and helmets and climbed trees. A bit scary, but manageable. The fourth day they informed us we were going to rappel from a 160-foot cliff—backwards. Wait a minute.

The morning of the "big climb" we had to drag several of the kids—members of the high school basketball team—from their tents. A good friend of mine, who shares my fear of heights, sat dejectedly outside his tent muttering, "This is my last day on earth and no one cares." He was serious.

We trudged up the backside of the cliff like condemned men on our way to execution. No one said a word. Occasionally you would see tears, from both men and women, but the long death march continued.

When we reached the top of the cliff, we walked out onto a narrow ledge and were told to sit down. From here we would literally jump off the mountain.

"Who would like to be first?" the mountain guide asked with a smile. The group sat silent. He might as well have asked, "Who would like to be the first to plunge to his death in screaming agony?"

I was single at the time and decided that I had lived a good life. I had no regrets that today it was ending. Rather than watching others fall to their deaths and end as a puff of smoke on the canyon floor, I decided to go first. As I stood trembling on the ledge of the mountain that sunny Colorado afternoon while mountain guides hooked me into belts and webbing, I had an occasion to review my life. My nineteen years had been good. My parents, friends, and family would miss me. But there would be life insurance, of course.

I walked toward the edge of the cliff as the guide gave me final instructions. "Face the mountain, lean over backwards, and begin feeding rope out through your right hand."

Lean backwards? What kind of sick mind would invent a sport like this? Inching my way to the edge of the cliff, I looked up at the sky. Ready or not, heaven would be receiving a new occupant in the next minute or two. I took a deep breath and leaned back. With my legs straight out in front of me at a perpendicular angle, I began lowering myself over a 160-foot sheer cliff.

I was just a few feet down the mountain when the thought suddenly struck me, "I must still be alive. No white lights or long tunnels yet." I let out a little more rope, then a little more, and finally began pushing away from the mountain, dancing and hopping down the side of the cliff. Elation swept through my soul. "I am alive! I'm actually still alive,"

By the time my feet touched the bottom of the canyon, I was transformed. Every cell and fiber of my body seemed to shout with exultation. When I unclipped my belts and looked up at what I had just done, I couldn't believe it was me. Bob Moeller – the coward of withering heights – was no longer afraid. In fact, I've gone on to enjoy rappelling on several occasions since then. So complete was my release that I later spent several summers roofing houses with my dad. I would sit on top of three-story homes and whistle as I nailed asphalt shingles to the roof.

What's the point of this story? Letting go of the idea "I married the wrong person" may be every bit as intimidating as walking backwards off a 160-foot cliff. It may mean that we have to face the fear of being intimate with the person we married. We may have to risk revealing who we are to another human being. We may have to be vulnerable to rejection and hurt in order to discover acceptance and love. Once we step over the cliff and discover we're still alive, it will mean changing the way we see ourselves and the person we married. When we face our fears and don't run from them, we do more than exist; we begin to really live.

The Will to Become the Right Person

The idea that we married the "wrong" person presupposes that there was a "right" person for us to marry but we didn't happen to guess correctly the first time around. To believe that we can find happiness with only one special person in all the universe seems a little far-fetched to me. Is there only one house in the entire nation you could live in and be happy? Only one type of car that could bring you satisfaction? One career?

We had a friend during college who was a native of India. His dating efforts in the United States proved frustrating and unsuccessful, so he returned to his home, and his relatives arranged for him to meet a lovely young woman. He had three hours to decide if he wanted to marry her. He did marry her and hasn't quit smiling since. Pure luck? We doubt it. He entered the marriage realizing, as Tevye said in *Fiddler on the Roof*, that they would learn to love each other.

In junior high I, Bob, had a crush on a girl, although I don't suppose she even knew it. I used to imagine what it would be like to walk her home from school, but my horn-rimmed glasses and bookworm images didn't interest her in the least.

I ran into her again almost twenty years later. I was a pastor making hospital calls, and she was a nurse. When I asked her about her life, a look of pain crossed her face. She and her former husband had married right out of high school and traveled across the country. They had two kids together before they divorced. She was now a single parent trying to make ends meet. While she was a pleasant person, we were very different people. In fact, I wondered what I had seen in her in the first place.

When I was a young man, I thought on several occasions I had found the right person. Somehow, they never got the message I was the right person for them. I remember dating one Miss Ideal only to learn she was seen passionately kissing another young man in the middle of campus. So much for that.

As time went on, I began to understand it was not a matter of me meeting the right person; it was me becoming the right person. As I matured in my self-knowledge and my relationship with God, I began to understand more about the type of person I wanted to spend my life with.

My definition of the right person also changed with the passing seasons of my life. Life is like that. Today you may be thinking you made the wrong choice, but let me encourage you, there are other seasons ahead. If you will soften your heart and begin building a marriage characterized by honesty, forgiveness, and acceptance, you may make a remarkable discovery. The individual you married can become the most precious person to you in all the world.

We strongly believe that God wants us to honor our marriage vows and spend our lifetime with the same mate. God would not ask us to do such a thing if he didn't build into the plan of marriage the ability to learn to love one another. Whether or not we believe we married "the right person," God can give us the capacity to become the right people for each other.

Bob once asked his parents how they made it through fifty years of marriage. They smiled and said, "We just decided we would." In the end, that's what marriage comes down to.

When we decide we have married the right person, we have.

A MODEST PROPOSAL
FOR A RESTART

I (Bob) was leaving the expressway one evening when a billboard caught my attention. A question was emblazoned there in huge, blue letters: "Diane, will you marry me?" I could only wonder how many times Dianes had rushed home, dialed their unsuspecting boyfriends, and shouted, "Yes!"

The billboard was clever and romantic, but it asked the wrong question. In fact, twenty-seven years ago when I asked Cheryl if she would marry me, I missed the point as well. Instead of posing the question "Will you marry me?" I should have asked "Will you be married to me?"

The difference is more than semantic, it is significant. Essentially the first question only asks, "Will you set a date, go through a ceremony, and sign a certificate with me?" The second asks, "Will you make a lifetime commitment to keep romance alive, to bear my burdens, to grow together in Christ, to show respect to me in front of others, and to work hard at keeping my dreams alive?"

That's a mouthful when you're down on one knee, but it comes closer to describing what a vital, growing marriage requires. If you're like us and asked —or answered—the wrong questions, the good news is it's not too late to propose again, whether you're the husband or the wife. We developed the following five questions as a great second proposal.

1. Will you keep romance alive in our relationship for a lifetime?

Women are often more interested in keeping romance alive than men are. During courtship a great deal of man's enthusiasm for buying flowers, writing thoughtful notes, and finding romantic places to eat is fueled by pent-up sexual energy. Once that sexual need is met in marriage and the novelty of the marriage relationship wanes, a husband's efforts to romance his wife may begin to fall off and feel like work.

The old adage is true: "If you want to feel romantic, act romantic." Writing thoughtful notes, spending time in deep conversation, and enjoying quiet walks together all build intimacy. The objective is not sexual intimacy, but emotional, relational, and spiritual intimacy as well.

It may feel like work at first but as we make the effort to keep romance alive in our marriage, feelings of closeness and attraction are rekindled.

2. Will you bear my burdens as I carry yours for a lifetime?

It's too bad that when we asked each other to marry us, we didn't ask for the privilege of shouldering each other's sorrows and difficulties. We should have, because bearing each other's burdens is a great part of what it means to be married.

Shortly after our first son was born, Cheryl's Uncle Charlie was killed in a collision just minutes after dropping Cheryl and the baby off. I stood by her in her hour of shock and grief.

Likewise, when Bob was laid off from his job, I (Cheryl) offered comfort and support. Once, when Bob appeared to be facing a debilitating illness, I promised I'd stay right by his side.

Neither of us bargained for such pain and difficulties the day we announced our engagement. But our willingness to bear one another's burdens has been one of the most important and meaningful experiences of our marriage. Paul encourages us in Galatians 6:2 to "Carry each other's burdens, and in this way you will fulfill the law of Christ." The law he refers to is the law of love, and burden bearing is at the very heart of marriage.

3. Will you promise to spend time with me to intentionally grow in Christ together?

Each of us should be reading the Bible regularly on our own, of course, but there is somethng uniquely powerful in reading the Bible to one another. In Ephesians, Paul uses the metaphor of "bathing" one another in truth, wisdom, and comfort of the Scriptures. Over time the pressures and problems of life take the luster off our souls. God's Word can restore a sense of freshness, purity, and vitality.

The intent, however, is not to misuse Scripture as a chisel to remake our spouses into our own image or as a spiritual paddle to punish our mates for the perceived imperfections and misbehavior.

Besides reading the Bible, we suggest reading a daily devotional together. We had the joy of writing a devotional for married couples called *Marriage Minutes.* A few minutes in the morning can help set you both on the same page all day long.

4. Will you treat me with respect in front of your friends and family members as I do the same for you?

We stayed one night in a home where the tension between the husband and wife was like an August atmospheric inversion. We could hardly breathe. The next morning we got up, packed our things, and politely excused ourselves from the danger zone.

Honoring one another before the world is nothing more than simple courtesy. But it involves restraining our emotions, swallowing hurtful words before they leave our mouths, and remembering that public humiliation leaves lifelong scars. Honor isn't simply the absence of put-downs; it's also the presence of affirmation and respect. It's as simple as being willing to get up and excuse ourselves from a meeting because our spouse dropped by the office or is on the phone.

When I (Bob) worked in an administrative setting, I left word with the receptionist that my wife should always be put through, regardless of what I was doing. It was a sign of respect. Likewise, I (Cheryl) have always refused to criticize Bob to my friends. I've been known to steer conversations in another directions rather than have the husbands for dessert.

Proverbs, chapter 31, advises husbands, "Give her the reward she has earned, and let her works bring her praise at the city gate." The same could be said for wives honoring their husbands.

If your marriage is suffering from respect-impairment, let me suggest you correct the problem through praise and affirmation, particularly in front of business associates, friends, and family. The rehabilitation of your love will be nothing less than a miracle.

5. Will you work hard at keeping my dreams alive?

The pressures of dealing with high mortgage payments, car repairs, youth sports, and church work can little by little wear us down. If we're not careful, we can end up so depleted by survival-fatigue that we allow our aspirations and visions to quietly die.

Cheryl graduated from college and went on to earn a master's degree. Yet she has primarily given herself to the incredible demands of raising our six children. I (Bob) have had to say to her over and over again, "I want to keep your dreams alive as well."

It's not too late to propose to your spouse again. The first time may have had all the flower power in the world, but this time you can have the sincerety of heart knowing full-well what you are pledging to one another.

Chapter Six

COMMUNICATION IS THE KEY

A COUPLE I (BOB) HAD NEVER MET BEFORE just showed up at my office one day. They were talking divorce. "The problem with Eli is that he simply won't communicate." The anger and bitterness in Megan's voice were unmistakable. "See for yourself," she taunted me, "Try having a conversation with him and see if you can get him to say more than fifty words."

I called Eli a few days later and invited him out to lunch. He gladly said yes. On the way to the restaurant, I rehearsed several questions I would ask him to see if I could get a conversation going. I entered the crowded lunchroom with verbal pliers in hand, ready to pull a conversation out of him if need be.

What happened next surprised even me. Once we were seated and had ordered, I asked Eli a simple question. For the next hour I rarely got a word in edgewise. He told me about his job, the family he grew up in, his college experiences, his car, and his love for Megan. He desperately wanted to save the marriage but had resigned himself that it was probably over.

On the way back to office I realized what was going on. It wasn't that Eli couldn't communicate; he had nearly talked my leg off. It was that Eli couldn't talk to Megan. Perhaps after losing one too many verbal firefights with his more articulate wife, Eli had decided life was safer in the bunker of silence and withdrawal.

WHAT MEN REALLY WANT FROM THEIR WIVES

Marriages can flounder for any number of reasons—money problems, emotional behavior, premarital sexual activity, in-law interference, and a variety of other causes. But they all share this characteristic: The couple can't talk to each other. They can't process their anger, resolve conflicts, or share their inmost feelings in an atmosphere of love, respect, and acceptance. As the pain of living together increases, and their ability to communicate diminishes, the marriage gradually dies.

Dr. Lois Ledierman Davitz, author of *Living in Sync: Men and Women in Love*, conducted a study of four hundred divorced men between the ages of twenty and forty-five, whose marriages had lasted anywhere from three months to twenty years. The study focused on finding the primary reason men divorce their wives. The results surprised the researchers. It was not problems with money, sex, children, or household duties that the men say broke up their marriages.

"What virtually every man in our study cited as decisive to the failure of the relationship was the lack of companionship," says Davitz. "In fact, the men who were planning to marry someone new invariably described her as 'my best friend.'"[1]

What goes into making a wife like a best friend?

"'Communication in friendship' is one of the first things men look for in a new relationship," say the researchers.[2] The problem is men see communication as a by-product of a shared activity, while women see it as the activity itself.

According to Davitz, and we believe she's right, the way to begin reconstructing communication in marriage is by doing things together. It may not be best to start your road back to reconciliation by scheduling a summit meeting in the living room where you two are going to hash out everything that's bothered you for the last two years or decades. As professional diplomats can tell you, wars often start after failed summits.

Instead, think back to your courtship days. Weren't many of your best conversations on dates where you did something you both enjoyed? Perhaps it was going to a park or concert, or skiing together. Your conversation grew out of your common activity.

"To be fair," Davitz says, "these [divorced] men probably shared this kind of camaraderie with their wives earlier in their relationships. Yet, somehow, as the stress of jobs, children and other responsibilities intruded, couples drifted away from this pattern of communication in friendship."[3]

WHERE TO START?

If the level of personal pain and frustration is so high at the moment, then we suggest you begin at a place where you once found success. There's an old Southern adage that says, "Dance with the one that brought you." If it was biking, listening to good music, or walking by the ocean that first drew you together and gave you an opportunity to share your hearts, then go back and do it again. Or find new activities that allow both of you to feel more at ease together. Let your communication grow spontaneously out of the things the two of you do together. We also suggest that you attempt to find ways to laugh together. Proverbs 17:22 says that "a cheerful heart is good medicine."

YOU HAVE A CHOICE

Communication is not some type of unusual gift or talent like being able to throw a football seventy yards or play cello with the Chicago Symphony Orchestra. Communication is more like keeping physically fit or going on a healthy diet. It is something you choose to do and develop. Anyone can have good communication in their marriage if they decide it is important and make consistent effort.

What are some practical ways to help your communication? We suggest these three daily tools:

1.   *Share two things that happen to you each day.* We suggest you share not only the facts of the event but strive toward communicating a feeling associated with what happened to you. How did you feel about it? You might want to limit the total time of your discussion to ten minutes in the beginning so as to not overwhelm the mate not naturally inclined to do this exercise.
2.   *Read a devotional book together each day.* It will give you a common experience and give you a platform to possibly discuss spiritually-natured things. If your spouse isn't agreeable to a spiritual devotional, read any kind of book together. It is still very likely to draw you together.
3.   *Pray together each day.* You cannot go to the Father in heaven together with your hearts and not be drawn closer to one another in the process. For those of you more timid in this area, Dr. Gary Chapman, author of *The Five Love Languages*, shares the art of silent prayer. Simply hold hands, close your eyes, pray silently, and say "Amen." You wait for your spouse to say "Amen," and you've just prayed together!

You can build on these simple starting points toward making communication a way of life. Remember, *everyone* can have good communication. It is a matter of will and consistent effort. We caution you not to think you are beyond these simple tools we have shared. If communication is not what you desire it to be in your marriage, we believe these three helps can be the consistent means of an open door between you each day.

SOLVING OUR CONFLICTS

Perhaps the most difficult aspect of communication in marriage is learning to solve conflicts. Although some couples seem to have a natural ability to resolve hard issues, most of us have to work at it. Unless we learn how to manage conflict in our relationship, it ends up managing us.

I (Bob) will never forget a scene I witnessed as a young boy in our neighborhood one summer day. I was playing in our front yard when I heard shouting start across the street. The front door to a neighbor's home burst open. A woman marched to her car, jerked open the driver's side door, then stopped to hurl one final epithet at her husband. Satisfied her insult had found its mark, she then got into the car. She cranked the engine, threw it into reverse, and hit the accelerator. The automobile shot backward out the driveway, careened across the street, and ran smack dab into a tree. The woman never got out of the car to inspect the damage but instead jammed the car into drive and screeched away down the street.

Obviously this couple was having problems communicating. A dented bumper and an ugly gash in the trunk of a tree were witnesses to that sad truth. But it was more than a reckless argument; it was an example of what conflict management experts call avoidance. While she obviously didn't avoid the tree, she did avoid staying at home to resolve the conflict. It was easier to flee than fight.

Avoidance is just one of the five different methods of communication that couples use when they're trying to resolve conflict. The other methods are competition, accommodation, negotiation, and collaboration.

Norman Shawchuck is a conflict management consultant who has written extensively on the ways human beings attempt to resolve conflict. He has catgorized and given names to each of these communication styles—the Shark, the Teddy Bear, the Turtle, the Fox, and the Owl.[4] They describe the predictable behavior of humans when faced with a conflict, and they may give you insight into yourself and your mate when you argue.

Meet Jaws in Person

1. The Shark (The Competitor). Sharks are competitors who see each marital argument, whether it's over the Visa Card or the electric bill, as a win or lose situation. And they intend to win. Sharks tend to be domineering, aggressive, and agreeable to any solution—as long as it's the one they want.

Sharks tend to get what they want one way or another. They're willing to use persuasion, power plays, or coercion to reach their goals. They will shout louder, sulk longer, or withhold sex. All is fair in love and war to a Shark. Watching a Shark in action isn't pretty, but being on the wrong end of their pearly white teeth is even worse, as any West Coast surfer will tell you.

Vanessa was a Shark. She controlled her husband and everyone else in her world with her temper. To keep the peace, and to save himself from the wrath of Mrs. Jaws, her husband would just give in whenever her gray fin started

There's a problem with a win/lose approach to communication. Even if you win, someone else loses. In marriage, that someone else happens to be the person who should be the most important, cherished person in your life. When a Shark is allowed to rule a marriage, subsurface anger builds, decisions are not enthusiastically carried out, and a dangerous dependency builds around the strong-willed individual, according to Shawchuck.

The subsurface anger is the part that worries me most. Our first year out of seminary we pastored a Midwestern church that had a considerable number of senior citizens, including Walter. Walter was known throughout the church as Mr. Milquetoast. He barely spoke above a whisper. He gave generously to offerings. He attended a Bible study on Thursday mornings at the church.

His first wife died, and in his eighties he remarried a lady who had a much stronger personality than he. We were shocked and horrified one night to learn on the evening news that his second wife had been brutally murdered with a crowbar. The hunt was on for the perpetrator of this heinous crime.

About a week later, just before turning in for the night, we again switched on the ten o'clock news. The lead story immediately caught my attention: "Tonight the police arrested a suspect in the murder of an elderly woman."

We expected to see a tough young guy with a four-day beard, perhaps flashing a gang signal, being led out of a squad car. Instead, the camera showed a hunched-over, eighty-eight-year-old man in bifocals and slippers, shuffling into police headquarters. It was Walter!

Walter was convicted of first-degree murder and sentenced to, yes, life in prison. The police believed the motive behind the killing was his simmering anger at his second wife for allegedly distributing some of his life savings to her children.

Although few couples resort to this extreme method of solving conflict, a win/lose dynamic is destructive to any couple's chances for long-term happiness. The person who loses all the time is eventually going to get sick of it.

Peace at Any Price

2. The Teddy Bear (The Accommodator). These people are easy to like because their life's ambition is to keep peace and make everyone happy. They see the world in terms of lose/win; that is, they are consistently willing to give up their rights to accommodate someone else's desires.

So what's wrong with that? Doesn't that make for an ideal partner? Actually, no. The problem with Teddy Bears is that they never solve problems' they just yield to other people to avoid any further conflict. These people are the "peace at any price" delegation. Just as history has shown that appeasement never leads to lasting peace, constantly surrendering principles and convictions in marriage leads ultimately to unhappiness and a breakdown of intimacy.

Using accommodation to solve conflicts in marriage ultimately gives the victors an unreal sense of their own rightness. And the Teddy Bears end up plagued by feelings of inauthenticity and falsehood for acting so cheerful and easygoing when in fact they are miserable and angry. They grow weary of frantically trying to keep the relationship together, which exacts a high price on their own emotional and spiritual health. The problems they've swept under the carpet for years come back to haunt them. Their self-esteem plummets from constantly accepting the blame for arguments and problems that were not their fault. Eventually, the emotional stuffing starts to fall out of a Teddy Bear.

Sybil was close to a nervous breakdown when we met her several years ago out West. Her husband traveled frequently and expected her to cope with the demands of sick children, running a house, and giving him time off to play with his buddies. If the baby cried during the nights, it was just expected that Sybil would be the one to get up. If Sybil's husband wanted to go away for the weekend fishing, it was up to her to pack the suitcase. If she ever objected to his carefree lifestyle, he would shout back, "Don't forget, I'm the one earning the money in this family." Meekly she would back down and work harder.

Sybil is a prime candidate for emotional exhaustion or an affair. Whenever she and her husband argue, he successfully manages to shift the blame for his own eternal adolescence and irresponsible behavior at her. Unfortunately, she accepts it. She honestly believes that's the loving thing to do. But they can't be happily married as long as Sybil continues her codependent behavior and allows him to play emotional tennis, constantly volleying guilt and blame onto her side of the court.

Let's Split the Difference

3. The Fox (The Negotiator). The Fox is a specialist at compromise. In marriages, Foxes are usually able to cut the tiramisu in such a way that it appears the other person got the biggest slice. They view relationships in terms of everyone-wins-a-little/everyone-loses-a-little. They genuinely want to see a compromise reached with their husband or wife, and they'll use a little gentle persuasion or manipulation to get the other person to sign on. Their bargaining skills are used to defuse potentially explosive situations in marriage, and for the most part they can do it with a smile. The problem with this particular style of communication and conflict resolution is that everyone goes away half-satisfied, the commitment to the solution is only half-hearted, and the same conflict will arise later because it's only half-solved.

Edward's in-laws didn't like him. When he and his wife would visit her parents, they would deliberately ignore him. They treated him as if he were an intrusion into their family. They refused to acknowledge any of his professional accomplishments. Edward told his wife about his deep hurt and sense of rejection. Instead of dealing with her parents in a direct fashion about their behavior, she suggested that he accompany her only every other time she visited them. That would cut in half the number of painful experiences he had to absorb from them.

That's the problem with compromise as a primary means of talking a problem out. The solution rarely gets to the root of the problem; it simply makes it less painful to live with.

What Problems?

4. The Turtle (The Avoider). These people are by no means an endangered species. They exist in marriages everywhere. When a problem pops up in marriage, their strategy is simply to pretend it doesn't exist. They may refuse to open bills they can't pay, or fail to return calls to angry neighbors. They see the world in terms of a lose/lose situation. They are so fearful of conflict that they become passive aggressive and withdrawn shadow figures.

Turtles are frustrating people to live with. They won't cooperate in defining the problem, or seeking a solution, or implementing an agreement. They have very little emotional investment in the relationship. Their emotional gears are stuck in neutral. When a husband or wife is trying to communicate with a Turtle, the Turtle will remain silent, or say little, or actually get up and leave the premises.

Norman Shawchuck tells the story of a couple he counseled who were having marital problems. The wife insisted on having all the family pets sleep in the same bed with them. There were at least two labs and a Persian cat on the queen-sized bed at all times. When the husband expressed his discontent, she just disregarded him. It was her method of avoiding intimacy with him. As long as there were representatives of the wild kingdom on their bed, nothing else too wild was going to happen.

Turtles tend to be heavy into denial. They say nothing when their partners make a reckless financial decision or come home boasting about the new woman at the office they took out to lunch. When Turtles find empty whiskey bottles in the garage, they simply throw them away and ask no questions.

Such passivity takes its toll on a marriage. Apathy eventually saps the energy and the excitement from the relationship. A famous celebrity trial involved a multi-millionaire husband who purportedly administered a lethal overdose of insulin to his wife to collect her estate and clear the way for marrying a mistress. Testimony at the trial confirmed the fact that his wife had told him he could keep the mistress if he wanted to, as long as he was discreet about it.

Perhaps the only statement more damaging to a marriage than "I hate you" is "I don't care."

Come, Let Us Reason Together

5. The Owl (The Collaborator). According to folklore, owls are wise creatures. Wise couples will adopt an "owlish" style of co-laboring toward solutions in their marriage. Owls desire a win/win solution to problems and disagreements. That's why they are willing to "co-labor," hence the term "collaboration," until mutually satisfying resolutions are reached to sticky and difficult issues.

The Owl is perhaps just the opposite of a Turtle. Owls are willing to stay up and talk a problem out rather than retreat to the solitude of a bedroom or night on the couch. They truly have the interests of both people at heart, and they see conflict as an opportunity to strengthen their marriage, not destroy it. When Owls solve problems, they tend to remain solved. They don't keep reappearing under some different guise. When a husband and wife collaborate and are committed to implementing the agreements they reach, they learn to trust each other, and they emerge a more thoroughly committed and satisfied couple.

The question in any marriage is not, "How can we avoid conflicts?" but "How can we learn to resolve them in a way that strengthens our marriage?" The answer to that is collaboration.

How then can a couple become Collaborators together? Let us suggest three helpful principles.

Get to the Real Issue

Seek to get to the heart of the conflict. When a couple approaches a problem in their marriage, they need to see it as an issue to be solved, not a person to be conquered. That requires sharing with each other all the true and relevant information that surrounds the issue. Misconceptions and assumptions have to be filtered out in favor of accurate and reliable facts.

Couples tend to exaggerate in an argument. "You've never remembered a single anniversary since we've been married!" "I always have to be the one to discipline the children!" "I can't think of a single nice word you've said to me this week."

An old proverb states, "Never say never and always avoid saying always." It's often difficult in the heat of battle to stop and sift out the wheat from the chaff or distinguish between the marble and the manure, but it's necessary if true conflict resolution is going to take place.

Collaboration requires putting those thoughts out of our minds. Such exaggerations aren't true, and they don't do anything to solve the problem. Dismiss them each time they try to grab hold of your thinking process. A Chinese proverb says, "That the birds of worry and care fly about your head, this you cannot change. But that they build nests in your hair, this you can prevent."

To gain useful data we need to ask each other questions such as, "What hurt you most about what I did?" "What's your greatest need at this moment?" "What's the issue behind this issue?" Counselors distinguish between the "presentation issue" and the "primary issue." A husband or wife will often bring up a problem that isn't the real issue, just because it's safer to talk about. It's a defense mechanism we use to make sure the other person is really open to our feelings and hurts before we disclose them. Or, we may be just too fearful to bring up the real subject, so we only hint at what we need.

For example, a spouse who is feeling like a failure at work may come home and ask why the house is such a mess or why the kids aren't dressed better. The other spouse might respond to the hurt or anger by complaining about the other's relatives. Couples who can't get past the presentation issue to discuss the primary issue will seldom solve their conflicts. Couples can get angry or upset over a relatively minor problem, but it's not the real problem. Successful communication in marriage requires putting our flamethrowers away and attempting instead to generate valid and useful information.

Respect Their Thinking

Give your mate the right to make free and informed choices. People don't enjoy having solutions forced on them. To build lasting harmony in a marriage, each person must be given the authority and freedom to make decisions as to how the problem will be solved.

Let's say the argument concerns housekeeping chores. It won't solve the issue for one person to announce, "From now on, you're doing the dishes and shopping for groceries, and I'm paying the bills online and doing the yard. And that's final." The only choice the other person has is to take it or leave it. Not very inviting. Far better to say, "Look, there's more work around here than either of us can handle alone. Let's discuss which chores each of us enjoys doing. Then, we'll work together on dividing up the remainder. What's your first choice of jobs? Then I'll share mine."

How important is it that couples learn to successfully negotiate smaller issues? Researchers at the University of Denver's Center for Marital and Family Studies set up mock living room labs and used sophisticated monitoring devices to study the behavior of couples trying to resolve conflict. Then director of the project, Dr. Howard J. Markman, claims that love and attraction don't naturally diminish over time; they are attacked and worn down by negative feelings that grow out of destructive fights.[5]

Dr. Clifford Notarius of Catholic University explains, "It matters less what couples fight about than how they fight about it."[6] I've had couples sit in my office and say, "It's hopeless. He (or she) is never going to change." That type of pessimism almost guarantees no progress.

Let us stress again, problems in marriage are issues to be solved, not people to be conquered.

Allow for Equal Input

People support solutions they have helped create. One-sided decisions or executive orders issued from the top don't cut it in a marriage. Both partners need to feel that they are an equal member of the decision-making process and their input matters.

The journal Bob worked for once printed a cartoon of ancient laborers groaning as they pulled a huge block of stone toward a pyramid. Riding atop the massive boulder was the Egyptian taskmaster. Below, the caption read his words to his forced laborers, "Remember fellas, we're all members of the same team."

We do believe the Bible's teaching that husbands should provide the spiritual leadership in the home, and wives should respect and submit to such spiritual initiatives and direction. We hear from wives how much they actually desire their husbands to provide leadership in vital areas of their family life. Yet, when it comes to solving the issues between them, partners should assume equal responsibility for resolving the problem and then implementing the solution together.

Brent and Gina were having problems with their cell phone bill. Each month it exceeded two hundred dollars. After several unproductive arguments over money, budgets, and phone calls, they decided to attack the problem together. Brent agreed to only talk to his friends on their evening and weekend hours, instead of calling them on his lunch hour. That brought discipline to the length and frequency of the calls. Gina agreed to stay in contact with her friends and relatives primarily with emails and IM instead of text messaging on the cell phone whenever she missed them. They set a target of one hundred dollars per month for cell phone service and then checked with each other frequently for support and accountability. Within a month's time the cell phone bill was under control. Why? Because Brent and Gina had both contributed to the solution, and as a result both were motivated to implement it.

Conclusion

Sooner or later, we all have to face the painful prospect of working through a major conflict. But conflict doesn't have to destroy a marriage. By choosing collaboration over competition, negotiating, avoidance, or accommodation, a couple can successfully navigate the difficult waters of disagreement.

How good and pleasant it is
when brothers and sisters
live together in unity!

- King David, Psalm 133:1

Chapter Seven

AREN'T MY NEEDS YOUR NEEDS?

SEVERAL YEARS AGO we were teaching a class for newly married couples. The discussion was discreet and lighthearted, but there was one unexpected interchange we've never forgotten.

"Men don't seem to understand," one wife said. "They think that just as long as they've satisfied their sexual needs, we're satisfied too. But when they're all finished, we're just ready to get started."

"Isn't that the sad truth?" piped up another woman, who was normally shy, quiet, and uncomplaining. No one could believe what she had just said. Her husband blushed seven shades of red.

The group was quiet for an instant, then it exploded with laughter. Several individuals laughed so hard they cried. The husband was speechless and undone. It took several minutes before anyone could say anything, and as soon as someone would attempt to change the subject, the laughter would start all over again. It was hopeless. As I glanced around the classroom, I noticed a slight tinge of guilt and embarrassment on more than one husband's face.

"The sad truth." It's a classic phrase that expresses the frustrations, confusion, and dilemmas many couples face when trying to understand the differences between them. Although challenging, we must give our best effort to trying to understand and fulfill the true needs of our spouse.

THE AIR WOMEN BREATHE

Several years ago NASA announced a novel experiment called *Biosphere II*. In a remote region of Arizona a large bubble was constructed. For two years scientists and others lived in an entirely self-contained, self-supporting world.

Everything needed to sustain life was either stored or grown inside the bubble. The goal was to study how future space explorers could create an environment that would sustain life and health in a hostile world.

As husbands we need to undertake a similar project in order to meet our wives' basic needs. We need to create a "biosphere" of love and nurture that allows our relationships to grow and stay healthy.

We believe that affection and conversation are the essential elements of love and nurture that a woman needs to thrive.

Non-Sexual Touch

I (Bob) once held a vow renewal ceremony at a weekend camp deep in the north woods in which I invited interested couples to come forward and recite again their marriage vows. The majority of the couples held hands and faced one another as they once again recited their sacred promises.

But I noticed one older man who refused to touch his wife or look her in the eyes. He just stood there, shoulder to shoulder with her, unable to reach out and display simple communication through loving touch. She left in tears as soon as the ceremony was over. He couldn't have hurt her any more deeply if he had wanted to.

Why? Although he mumbled the vows, more important to her than the words was the need to feel his affirmation through his willingness to move toward her in touch. His awkwardness with physical displays of tenderness kept him from meeting a basic need in her life. It likely had done considerable damage to their relationship through the years.

Husbands need to understand that women never grow tired of being held, touched, kissed, or hugged. To wives it is a sure sign they are valued and cherished. Conversely, failing to show affection may be one reason many husbands are rebuffed when they jump into bed at the end of the day and send signals they'd like sex.

Several summers ago we witnessed a ride at the Minnesota State Fair called *The Ejection Seat*. It was a bungee launch rather than a bungee jump. Two long bungee cords are stretched down and attached to a secure, double-seated bench on the ground. Two brave (and slightly crazy) people allow themselves to be strapped in. On command the fair workers release the cord holding the bench down, and the occupants are hurled in their seat twelve stories straight up into the sky. They actually go from zero to seventy miles per hour in less than a second.

(We considered trying the ride but decided instead on the tunnel of love.)

Now bungee launching may be great fun for thrill seekers, but when husbands try going from zero to seventy in the bedroom, it's no amusement. Instead, they need to take time all throughout the day to display affection to our wives.

Conversation

Wives need not only affection but conversation to build intimacy with their spouse and thus fulfill their emotional needs. Because a husband is often not as verbally skilled as his wife, learning to converse with her can be difficult. Again, as one marriage researcher discovered, *men see communication as a by-product of a shared activity* whereas *women see communication as the activity itself.* So one key for men and women to connect verbally is to talk during the course of doing an activity together on a daily basis—such as cleaning the yard or going for a walk.

Whereas men use communication to share information and ideas, women also use it to connect emotionally and to bond with others. If a husband is willing to try the same thing - to connect and bond with his wife through conversation—he will meet one of their basic needs. Conversation will reduce the sense of distance and detachment that can impair intimacy.

Meaningful communication involves well-chosen words. Remember the classic literary story of Cyrano de Bergerac, the homely, awkward Frenchman with an incredibly large nose? He was in love with a ravishingly beautiful woman yet so ashamed of his features that he didn't dare to confess his feelings in person. Instead he started writing he love letters. But to avoid rejection, he signed another man's name.

Over the months his love letters proved so eloquent, so romantic, so tender he completely swept the woman off her feet. Sadly, though, she believed it was the other man who had won her. Poor Cyrano was left languishing in the shadows.

When the day finally came that she learned the truth, a remarkable thing occurred. Rather than rejecting the homely Frenchman, she had been so moved by his words that she overlooked his nose and fell smashingly in love with him. She had fallen in love not with his face, but with his soul.

There's a lesson to be learned from homely Cyrano. If men wish to create an atmosphere in which a woman's love will flourish, they need to learn to communicate tender, heartfelt, meaningful, and romantic words.

Avoid Being Mr. Fix-It

Speaking complimentary words is only half of conversation; the other half is listening. Women not only want to be heard, *they want to be understood.* Unfortunately, men often misinterpret what women are saying when they share their feelings. Men assume women are asking them to "fix" their problems. Nothing could be further from the truth.

Consider this wife's efforts to be heard and her husband's response. She begins the conversation by sharing with him the low point of her day:

"Dear, the car died in the intersection this afternoon. I just sat there for ten minutes...."

"Did you hold the accelerator down to the floor and count to three like I told you to do?"

"Yes, but it didn't work. Horns were blaring, the baby was crying...."

"I've told you before, don't panic when the car dies. Just do what I say. Hold the accelerator down and count to three. Then turn the key. It should start."

"You're not listening."

"What do you mean 'not listening'? Did you try to start the car just the way I told you?"

"It wasn't just the car. Oh, never mind."

"Hey, where are you going? What did I say? I was only trying to help."

Now let's try that same conversation but add listening and empathizing with her feelings about the incident.

"Dear, the car died in the intersection this afternoon. I just sat there for ten minutes...."

"Oh, I'm sorry. I hate that when it happens to me."

"You can say that again. I can't tell you how embarassing it was. Horns were blaring, the baby was crying...."

"It's frustrating and humiliating."

"Yes. I wanted to just take the baby and walk away from it. I pumped the accelerator as you suggested, but it didn't work."

"Well, I'm just glad you and the baby are safe."

"That was my worst fear, that someone would hit us."

"Thank heaven no one did."

"What's causing the problem dear?"

"I'm not certain. Will you please take it in and have it checked out?"

"Sure."

"Did the rest of your day go better?"

"Fortunately yes."

Now what is the difference between the two conversations in our simple example? Which approach conveys that he was listening? Which creates a "biosphere" where a woman's needs are met?

Women certainly have other needs as well such as financial support and their husbands' loving leadership in the home. But affection and conversation are two primary elements in meeting a woman's needs. A husband who provides that atmosphere will find it significantly improves their marriage and, as a result, his wife will be far more likely to reach out and fulfill his significant needs as well.

THE IDEAL GIFT FOR YOUR HUSBAND

Every year at Christmas retailers offer help to wives who are searching for the perfect gift for "the man who has everything." We could save such dedicated shoppers a great deal of time and money by sharing the truth about what their husbands need most: sexual fulfillment and companionship. If affection and conversation are the elements of the "biosphere" women operate best in, then a fulfilling sex life and companionship are the air men breathe.

A Blessing or a Curse?

It's easy to misunderstand or misinterpret a man's sexual needs. We've heard wives complain that "all my husband wants is sex" or that "he's oversexed." What some wives fail to understand is that the sexual drive in a male is a very natural, strong force, which is one powerful means of domesticating an otherwise independent creature.

To be sure, some men are guilty of using sex as a means of controlling their wives. We object to abusive, degrading, or violent male behavior under any circumstances. If that's present in your marriage, we suggest you contact your pastor and seek professional counseling immediately.

But the sexual needs of husbands can serve several positive and redemptive purposes in marriage. To begin with, sexual desire helps steer adult males toward a marriage commitment. An exhaustive study performed at the University of Chicago stated that curiosity/readiness for sex and physical pleasure is the reason 73 percent of men had their first intercourse (while only 23 percent of women gave this reason)[1]. It's our conviction that this curiosity and readiness for sex is an incentive toward marriage. The same guys who loved eating pizza at two in the morning, going fishing for a week in the north woods, and playing football all Saturday are willing to suddenly turn that energy toward establishing a home, providing a living, and sharing their lives with a wife. Why? They want sex from their spouse.

Obviously a marriage needs to be built on much more than a male's sexual desires, but give credit where credit is due. When male sexual energy is directed toward the institution of marriage, it contributes to the stability of our society and the creation of long-lasting, commited relationships.

A Procreative Force

God also gives men a strong sexual instinct to favor procreation. Few ancient or prescientific cultures understood that conception is possibly only a few days a month for a woman. What would have happened to the human race if husbands had been given a weak sex drive and sex twice a year had suited them just fine? Would the human race have survived or prospered?

Perhaps, but the sexual needs of a husband and wife are a positive force in fulfilling the Genesis directive to "be fruitful and multiply."

The Bond that Frees

The final benefit of a male's need for sexual fulfillment is the bonding that occurs. Something mysterious, intimate, and lifechanging occurs in the act of sexual intercourse. A "oneness" of flesh leads to a "oneness" of spirit. When the other necessary elements of a loving marriage are present, frequent and regular sexual intercourse strengthens the bond. It ties yet one more cord around the heart.

Nor does a male's need for sexual fulfillment diminish much with time. The University of Chicago study reported that 66 percent of men ages fifty to fifty-nine engage in sex a few times a month of more, similar to the 64 percent of men ages eighteen to twenty-four[2]—despite the fact men supposedly reach their sexual peak at age nineteen. As a result of the husband's lifelong need for sexual fulfillment, the positive bond it creates can be reinforced over an entire lifetime.

When the male need for sexual fulfillment is lived out under the plan of God, it is a blessing, not a curse, both to society and to the marriage relationship.

Will You Be Their Buddy?

Besides sexual fulfillment men also need a recreational companion. Often men aren't good at verbalizing what they need, but let us say it on behalf of all men.

Your husband wants you, his wife, to be his buddy. We don't care if a man is twelve years old or sixty, he still wants a friend to do things with.

Let's say your husband comes in the door and says, "Honey, would you come out and help me with the yard work?" You're thinking, "What did I ever do to deserve such a Don Juan?"

But let us translate what he's really saying.

"Dear, sometimes it's a lonely world for a husband. I'd like you to do something I used to ask my buddies to do with me when I was single—work on a project with me. So even though it means interrupting what you're doing, just your being beside me and talking to me will help me feel like I've got a friend."

Wives, if you knew your husbands were acutally saying that to you, wouldn't it change your minds about going fishing, watching a game on television, or going to Home Depot together? If it's conversation you want, what better thing to do than get in a small boat and go fishing for the day? After all, where's he going to go that you won't? You've got him all to yourself for eight hours.

Don't underestimate your husband's need for a friend. A group of four hundred divorced men who were planning to remarry were asked what they liked most about their new fiancees. The number one answer was, "She's my best friend."[3]

CONCLUSION

Some time ago we heard an author on the radio share the story of the near demise of his marriage. He loved golf and spent most of his discretionary time of the greens. As his marriage disintegrated, he became more and more demanding that his wife meet his needs. If she would just let him live the way he wanted, everything would work out just fine, he reasoned.

Eventually he realized they were on the verge of divorce. He went home, put his golf clubs in the closet, and told her he was now interested in meeting her needs. At first she didn't believe him. But over time, as he put her first in his life and learned what she really needed from him, their relationship changed. Their love was renewed. He couldn't wait to get home to her. Their sexual relationship heated up again.

One day his wife met him in the hallway and handed him his golf clubs.

"What are you doing?" he asked.

"I want you to go play golf," she smiled. "It's been three years since you last played. I want you to go and enjoy yourself."[4] When he decided to meet her needs, it awakened a response in her to meet his.

It's a simple strategy, but it transformed their marriage. It can transform yours as well.

Chapter Eight

MAKING WAR, NOT LOVE

ONE SPRING OUR DAUGHTER walked in the house and said, "Dad, there are bubbles coming from the ground in the backyard."

"There are what?" I (Bob) asked. I went outside and was directed to a damp spot just behind our back wall. Sure enough, every time we ran water in the kitchen sink or turned on the washer, bubbles would come up as if it were the original set of the 1950's Lawrence Welk Show.

While I'm not likely to host *Extreme Home Makeover*, I know a costly repair job when I see one. Bubbles in the back yard could only mean one thing —money. And lots of it.

I called a neighbor who is a plumbing contractor. "Tom, I've got bubbles in my backyard. And it smells something awful."

"I'll check it out when I come home from work," he offered.

Tom is great guy. He showed up that same night before supper. Shovel in hand, he walked into our backyard, took one whiff of the bubble geyser, and said, "I bet it's your grease pit."

"My what?"

"Grease pit. They installed these after World War II in houses like yours. If they get plugged up, it can cause real trouble. Stand back; this won't be pretty." Tom dug his shovel into the ground, and we heard a clunk. "Yup," he smiled, "you've got one. This thing captures all the grease from kitchen or laundry." He dug a short while longer and unearthed a large metal manhole cover, which he pried off with a crowbar.

Underneath was the worst looking, most foul smelling, gray liquid you've ever encountered in your life. "This stuff is even worse than sewer water," he grinned. He didn't need to tell me. Already my sinuses had been thoroughly scalded.

"What do we do now?" I asked, my eyes running red.

"We'll find where the line is blocked and rout it out. But first we have to pump some of this stuff out."

"Where?"

"Oh, a little on your back yard won't hurt anything," he said. Before I knew it, he had dropped a pump the size of a blender into the gray cesspool and started it up. In less than ten seconds, awful looking, murky, mucky, rank, hair-curling liquid was spewed onto my lawn.

"Tom, when does this stuff go away?" I asked.

"Oh, two or three good rainstorms should take care of it," he said calmly.

I looked up. There wasn't a cloud in the sky. Joggers running by our house slowed down, sniffed, then broke into a sprint.

"Uh, oh," said Tom. "It isn't looking so hot for the good guys."

"What's wrong?" I asked, now visualizing semitrailers pulling into our driveway and unloading several backhoes to dig up our entire yard.

"I think the line has collapsed somewhere near the basement. We'll have to go through the concrete floor," he said.

Tom said there was nothing more he could do at the moment, so we buried the grease pit for the night. That evening as the smell of rotting grease wafted through our open windows, I aksed myself what I had done to deserve this.

Considering the possible time and expense involved in fixing the problem, I mentally rehearsed my options. First, I could put the house up for sale and practice saying with a straight face, "Smell? What smell?" Second, I could leave the air conditioner on for the next two years and forget about the backyard. Or third, I could face the stench head on. It could mean tearing up the basement floor, emptying our bank account, and waging war with gray, fetid chemicals most international treaties ban. But sooner or later I might win.

The next morning I made my choice and called my neighbor. "Tom, go ahead and do what you need to do in the basement because we've got to deal with the grease pit. I'll be here Saturday to help you if you need it."

"No," he said bravely, "it would be better if the house were empty when Idid this." We both knew the smell could get ugly.

That Saturday I had a speaking engagement that took me away for the day.

Late in the day I called Cheryl to ask about the bill. "Well, tell it to me straight. How much did this set us back?"

"You won't believe this," she said. I braced myself, wondering if there was a debtor's prison in our state. "Tom found a simple solution to the problem and was able to repair it in just a few hours."

It was as if a presidential pardon had just been granted. The grease pit had been emptied and our lives could go on.

The anger between a husband and wife often resembles that bubbling grease pit in our backyard. Such anger doesn't subside or disappear by ignoring it. If it isn't dealt with, it will contaminate all aspects of the relationship.

Getting rid of toxic anger requires digging up the problem, draining off the ugly fluid of animosity and antagonism, and allowing honesty, love, and forgiveness to repair the damage. Fortunately, we aren't in this struggle alone. God himself is willing to work in our lives and relationships to replace hostility and resentment with grace and reconciliation.

FOUR TECHNIQUES
TO DEAL WITH ANGER

So what do we do with our anger in a relationship? Proverbs 29:11 says, "A fool gives full vent to his anger, but a wise man keeps himself under control." As we discussed in the last chapter, the goal is to develop communication skills that will allow us to process that anger. It's not healthy to bury feelings, because when we do, we bury them alive.

That's why we must learn the principle of speaking the truth in love to each other. Some people are naturally blunt and have no problem laying the truth on someone else, but they overlook people's feelings. The results can be devastating.

I (Bob) was once publicly reprimanded for something I had overlooked. The person was right; I had failed. But the public nature of the rebuke left scars. That conversation should have taken place behind closed doors.

Other people are inclined to show love but have trouble sharing the truth because they don't want to hurt someone else's feelings. The relationship is stymied because they can't bring themselves to share what's really on their heart.

For anger to be drained out of a relationship requires both truth and love. As Bill Hybels writes, "We must be willing to risk chaos to achieve community." We risk confusion, controversy, and even pain in order to achieve reconciliation.

We're not wired to do that naturally. We flinch at the idea of opening up and sharing the hurt we are carrying inside. What if the other person blows up, falls apart, or walks out?

But we must take those risks, in a spirit of love, if we are to deal with our anger. Sometimes we have to disturb the peace, because it's a false peace, if we're going to find lasting meaning and contentment in our relationships.

Here are four of the worst ways to process anger and hide truth in a relationship:

1. Dropping Hints

This approach is used by husbands and wives who don't have the courage to tell someone else their behavior is hurtful or driving them up the wall. They choose instead to drop ever-so-subtle hints. We all see right through such game playing. The result is usually a worse confrontation than if we had dealt straight in the beginning.

When a couple starts dropping hints about their dissatisfaction with their sexual relationship, it can come out as sarcasm. "How about if I have my needs met first so I can go to sleep and leave you frustrated this time?" Or, "I sure miss the days when you seemed interested in making love, but I guess we all get older, don't we?" Even under the veil of humor, dropping hints can be a disguise for deep-seated animosity. It's not funny, or healthy.

2. Manipulation

This approach is to get people to do what we want by outmaneuvering them. We paint them into a corner where they have no choice but to yield. Perhaps we use sexual or emotional blackmail, or sulk around the house, or pull the covers over our head and turn away when our partner makes a move toward us.

We all rebel at being manipulated. We get angry when people try to get us to change without saying what's on their mind or what they need. In the end, it may drive us to the very behavior the other person is trying to change.

3. Guilt tripping

Comedians love to parody the mother who calls her son the night before Mother's Day and says, "No, son, you don't need to take me to lunch tomorrow.

After all, who am I? Just your mother. Never mind the fact I was in labor fifty-six hours with you. So what? Forget the fact I gave up the flower of my youth to raise you. Or that I cleaned houses to put you through college. No, you go out with your wife tomorrow. I'll just go down to the 7-11 and buy myself a rose and watch Jeopardy."

Some marriages operate on the same high-octane guilt. One person has learned the art of making the other person feel so obligated, so indebted that only a grubworm would say no.

Using guilt to control a spouse can destroy the spontaneity and joy of a sexual relationship. "Go ahead, even though I'm not feeling well. I know you have needs." Or, "If you really loved me, you'd cancel your golf game and stay home to make love. But I can't ask you to do that, can I?" Guilt and passion are poor roommates. One or the other eventually has to move out.

4. Intimidation

Perhaps the most dehumanizing alternative to speaking the truth in love is this raw, ugly, crass use of power to get what we want. Shouting, threats, insults, and even violence are pulled out of the drawer to control the other person. It destroys the adult-to-adult nature of a marriage and turns it into a parent-to-child relationship.

When I, Bob, was a fifth grader, my family went camping with a group of professionals from my father's place of employment. A woman in the tent next to us walked over and asked if she could borrow a couple of dollars to buy milk at the camp grocery store. My parents gladly helped her out. About an hour later shouts erupted from her tent. Then her husband appeared at the door of our trailer and handed the money back to my parents. "She isn't supposed to ask for money," he said, sounding like a father who had just caught his child misbehaving. "She can get all the money she needs from me." The wife was so embarrassed she virtually hid in the tent for the remainder of the weekend. I was not surprised to hear they were divorced a few years later.

Sex can often be used to intimidate a spouse. "If you don't start responding better to me in bed, I may have to start looking elsewhere." Or, "Don't come near me. If you do, I will move out." When anger takes the form of intimidation, one spouse may get his or her way, but ultimately the marriage is in serious trouble. It's only a matter of time until the meltdown occurs.

IT'S TIME TO RISK CHAOS
TO ACHIEVE INTIMACY

If each of these four methods is ineffective in dealing with anger in marriage, what should spouses do? We are back to the only real alternative people have to process their anger, which is to speak the truth in love. Ephesians 4:15 tells us, "Instead, speaking the truth in love, we will in all things grow up into Him who is the Head, that is, Christ."

But truth comes hard for many people. If you were raised in a home with fighting, alcoholism, sexual abuse, or other forms of destructive behavior, you learned the one rule that ran the house: Never, ever, speak the truth. Never ever say that dad was a drunk. Never tell anybody what your uncle did to you when you were alone together. Never speak up and say that you hated your parents' fighting.

If you were never given permission to discuss your feelings or the truth (not at least without paying an enormous price), you just buried them all – alive. As a result, today you may be carrying a mixture of rage, guilt, sadness, low self-esteem, and a fear of intimacy. Such unresolved anger effectively destroys your life of intimacy.

It's time to change. It's time to risk chaos in the context of love. How can we talk about painful things without emotionally stabbing the other person? Let us offer several positive steps. If we're going to share some potentially painful things with our husband or wife, we need to follow some simple guidelines.

Start with Affirmation

First, we need to ground our comments by affirming our relationship. "Natalie, my marriage to you means more than anything else in life. I want so much to be sensitive to you and enrich your life. I don't want anything to take away from our relationship. That's why I need to talk about our love life and the things that are creating anger and hurt inside of me."

Don't Make Accusations

It's vital to make observations instead of accusations. Just because we think something is true, doesn't make it true. Sometimes we can honestly misinterpret situations or behavior and come to an entirely wrong conclusion. We may not understand all that is behind our spouse's behavior or decision.

Accusations hurt, particularly when they're wrong: "You won't make love to me tonight because you're frigid (or impotent)."

Consider how this statement could be rephrased to make an observation, not an accusation: "I sense you're not in the mood for romance tonight. Are you feeling stressed out?"

The dynamics of the situation have changed from an argument between prosecuting attorneys to a quiet conversation between friends.

Use "I" Statements

Another key element of speaking the truth in love is the use of "I" statements. An "I" statement merely describes your feelings or reactions to another person's behavior. It passes no judgments and makes no pronouncements on the other person's character.

Take the example of Hunter and Kirsten, whose sex life had diminished recently. It had been ten days or more since Hunter showed any interest in his wife. One night Kirsten came to bed and sent the clear signal she wanted love. But Hunter turned on *Conan O'Brien* instead and watched television until he fell asleep.

At breakfast the next morning Kirsten decided to broach the painful, but delicate subject. By using "I" statements she made this positive encounter: "Hunter, darling, I need to talk to you. I'm not certain how to interpret your behavior lately, but let me share how it's impacting me. When you show no sexual interest in me, I feel unwanted, unloved, unattractive. When you choose to watch television rather than make love to me, I feel hurt and humiliated, particularly when I ask you to make love to me. I don't know what you may be dealing with right now, but I'd like to talk about it."

This opened the door for Hunter to respond: "Oh, Kirsten, I'm sorry. I haven't meant to hurt you. I love you and want you just as much as ever. I guess I haven't been the same since I learned they're planning to close our office next year. I've just been feeling so depressed lately I'm not interested in anything. All my years of service there suddenly seem so worthless. I'm sorry, honey. I guess I never stopped to consider how my behavior might be affecting you."

Kirsten created a safe environment for discussion by pointing out specific behaviors that were troubling her and by describing their impact on her life. She never accused Hunter of anything. She commented only on actions, steering away from character assaults or accusations.

Because Hunter was not in the position of defending himself, he was free to share his feelings and to clarify his intentions. That led to the discovery that Hunter was probably suffering from a mild depression, which often drains the energy from a person's sex drive. Hunter was not experiencing negative feelings toward Kirsten, but rather was having trouble coping with life at the moment. He was grieving over his impending loss of a job, and that grieving took the form of depression.

Their ability to communicate led them to seek help for the real problem – Hunter's depression. As a result, they were soon able to resume a life of fulfillment and happiness, treasuring the gift of sexuality they were able to offer each other.

PAROLED FROM PRISONS OF OUR OWN MAKING

When we feed our anger and fear or our appetite for revenge, we confine ourselves to a dungeon of our own making. The irony is this. We can find freedom and happiness in our relationship just as soon as we choose to deal with anger in a positive way. If we don't, we may eventually start sleeping in other parts of the house, or with someone else. Anger and unresolved tension almost always result in a discontented sexual relationship as well. We end up making war, not love.

Is there a way to restore passion in a marriage where the fire seems nearly extinguished? Can couples renew their love life? Definitely. In the next chapter we'll discover the true aphrodisiacs of marriage, the mysterious elements that can bring heat and intensity back to a cold and apathetic sexual relationship. Chances are you haven't read about them in supermarket tabloids or heard them discussed on a cable talk show. But the formula is as old as marriage itself.

Note: For a deeper discussion on anger, we suggest Dr. Gary Chapman's *The Other Side of Love: Handling Anger in a Godly Way*, Moody Publishers.

Chapter Nine

YOU CAN'T HAVE IT ALL

WE'LL NEVER FORGET THE DAY we found our dream house. We were new to Chicago and had been renting for less than a year. With four children six years old and younger, it was obvious we needed more space. So we started driving through new construction sites and subdivisions to look for a new home. All over our county new housing developments were popping up like mushrooms in a damp Kentucky cave.

After weeks and weeks of touring models, looking over floor plans, and asking sales representatives if there wasn't one too many zeros on the price tag, we at last found the place we had been dreaming of. The subdivision had a lovely, idyllic, rural-sounding name like "Country Meadows." (Actually it was next to a cemetary and a four-lane road, but developers and Realtors are sometimes gifted with vivid imaginations.) When we discovered that the home was "almost" in our price range, we were ecstatic. A few weeks later we signed a purchase agreement, adding a fourth bedroom, a fireplace, and improved carpeting on top of the base price.

Soon construction began. We went almost every day to watch them build our little house by the tollway. Slowly our dream dwelling took on shape, first with poured concrete and blocks, then studs and roofing, and finally walls and appliances. It was beautiful. It was perfect. It was expensive.

It was the hottest August in a hundred years when we moved in. Once we were done paying all the extra costs involved in a real estate closing (we were charged for walking in the door, using their chairs to sit in, being alive) we didn't have a penny to spare. But the house was ours.

As we thundered up to our new residence in the rented Ryder moving truck, we looked with pride over our new home and our front yard—which was nothing but black dirt. "That's right," we remembered, "the house doesn't come with a lawn. Oh well, that will have to wait." We had so little money left over after closing that other items (like curtains) had to come first.

As the weeks went by, we discovered more hidden costs in setting up a new household. There were rugs to buy, mailboxes to install, shower curtains to hang, and on and on. Meanwhile, as other neighbors has their lawns professionally seeded or sodded, we waited. And waited.

Winter mercifully arrived, camouflaging our bare front yard with a blanket of snow. But spring eventually followed, and we still had no funds to put in a lawn. It started to get a little embarrassing. We prayed for an answer to our bald yard.

Heaven must have heard my prayers because I received an answer almost immediately. Weeds! Green weeds. Tall green weeds. The same color as grass. Sensing an opportunity, I (Bob) brought our lawn mower out of hiding and mowed on a diagonal so it would give the appearance of professional lawn care. With head held high I roared across the yard back and forth, back and forth. It was exhilarating. Waving at the neighbors next door, I said, "Beautiful spring day, isn't it?"

Despite the temporary lawn fix, we knew our financial situation was worsening. The day finally came when we sat down and had "the talk." With taxes and assessments about to go up, with utility payments larger than we had expected in our much larger home, and with no money for an authentic lawn, we were stressed out. We considered our options. We discussed Cheryl getting a job but rejected that ideas for a variety of reasons—the most obvious being our four children at the time. We discussed Bob getting a second job. He was already working a full-time job and commuting close to an hour each day. We hardly had time alone as it was.

Unless we could solve our financial dilemma, we would be forced to seek additional employment and become a "quality time" family. To put it another way, we were facing the disintegration of our life together as a family and couple.

The cost of keeping our dream home and the pace of life it demanded had become a nightmare. We agonized over the decision. We prayed long and hard about it. We asked the advice of others. In the end we made what we believe, to this day, was the right choice.

Just nine months after moving into our dream home, Bob pounded a "For Sale by Owner" sign into our front yard (into the weeds to be more precise). We advertised in a tiny circular where you recieve a free ad if you send in a recipe (we chose 'Dirt Pie' appropriately enough.) We sold our home in less than a month and purchased a forty-five-year-old home exactly half the size. Not only that, but our smaller home had a lawn. A real lawn with real grass. (The Realtor was baffled by Bob's over-excitement about that feature.)

But we didn't stop there. We also sold our new minivan and bought two used vehicles, whose combined mileage was the distance from the earth to the moon. We cut costs wherever we could. In short, we did a radical downsizing.

But as a result, we didn't have to put our children in day care. Cheryl didn't have to take a job outside our home. Bob didn;t end up with a pacemaker. The bills started to diminish, our taxes went down, and our lives began to work again. Best of all, we had time once again to be parents, friends, and lovers we wanted to be.

LIVING IN REALITY

Perhaps the most needed wisdom for overstressed (and undersatisfied) couples in this generation is this, "You can't have it all." It's painful to hear; we don't want to accept it, but it's the truth.

Most of us simply can't afford all the homes, toys, vacations, and entertainment we want and still have time for our children, church, extended family, friends, and most of all our spouse. But the possibility that the current generation might enjoy less material prosperity than their parent's generation is simply unacceptable to most people today.

Let's face reality. Life is a series of trade-offs. We all must choose between having this and sacrificing that. The reason life gets busier and busier and busier is that we believe we're the exception. We think we can have it all if we will just work a little harder and a little smarter.

I watch the result of that type of thinking on Saturdays and Sundays in our overly busy little community. On Saturdays worn-out moms and dads stand on the sidelines of a soccer field, many still wound tight from the week. Little Sarah on the other team lets a goal get by, and her parent/coach screams, "Didn't you see that coming! Where's my defense? Wake up!" Meanwhile, Sarah, who's supposed to be having a good time, is blinking back tears.

At lunchtime our hyped-up, busy family will sometimes jump in the car and head over to McDonald's. Standing next to me are strangers, faces tense, trying to make sense of the different menu items being shouted at them by the kids. When young Calvin spills ketchup on his cute little Gymboree pants, the mother loses it. "Now, look at what you've done. Do you know how much those cost?

We'll have to go home and change." Meanwhile Calvin has forgotten that the reason his mother worked so hard all week was so he could enjoy wearing clothes she thinks are acceptable on the cute-o-meter.

For many stressed-out parents it's on the next event, and the next. They seem so desperate, yes, desperate to enjoy their day. The result is manic afternoons of people rushing from activity to another, searching for the joy and relaxation that eluded them all week long and trying to squeeze it in before the work starts again Monday morning.

Take one of these couples and put them in bed late Saturday night after such a self-imposed hectic day. They spent a ton of money (some on credit), the kids fought with each other in the car all afternoon, and now they are both frazzled. Is it any wonder that current surveys show a considerable number of married people having sexual relations only a few times a month?

If we don't decide as a couple that nurturing our marriage and family life us important to us, and then take the radical steps necessary to carve out time together, love isn't going to happen. The years will go by, the kids will grow up, and we'll come to the end of it all and ask why? Why did we push so hard?

CHOOSE TO LIVE, CHOOSE TO LOVE

So how does a very busy couple create time to nurture their marriage and keep their intimacy alive and healthy? Let us make a few suggestions:

1. Decide who you love is more important than what you own.

To put an entire lifetime in perspective, let me recommend you visit the home of an elderly person in the near future. They'll enjoy the visit, you'll encourage them, and it will give you an idea of how fast life goes by.

Pay particular attention to the pictures on their walls or on top of their piano. Chances are you'll see an old black-and-white photograph of their wedding. Then you may find slightly faded color pictures of their children with hair styles and glasses from decades ago. You might also discover a menagerie of pictures of smiling grandchildren—some missing teeth, others covered with freckles.

They likely own all their furniture, car in the driveway, and possibly their home. But is that what they now value most in the world? We doubt it. It's the faces in those pictures and the relationships they represent that are more precious to them than anything on earth. If they could turn back the clock, do you think they would choose to earn more money or to spend more time with their children who are now grown and gone? You know the answer.

So what does this have to do with enhancing our relationship with our spouse? For some of us, our marital lives will only improve when we do a serious moral inventory of our life values. If we can't say that loving people, especially our spouses, is more important than having things, we have distorted and short-sighted values. It's time to change.

Let us warn you, change won't come easily. Every fiber and muscle in our bodies will shout, "No! You can't give all this up! Your possessions make who you are. What will other people think? You'll be a loser. A no one!" But if we are going to create the one item we all must have in order to enjoy frequent and meaningful interactions—time—then we are going to have to make some hard choices.

We may need to change jobs. We may need to be by-passed for some promotions. We may need to sell our homes and buy less expensive ones. We may need to move to an area where the cost of living is lower and settle for fewer perks.

But if we really believe who we love is more important than what we own, few sacrifices will be too much. And the dividends? Time to lie together in bed simply cherishing the moment. Time to walk hand in hand down the street after supper. Time to teach a class at church. Time to read to our kids at night or wrestle with them on the floor or spray them with a garden hose on a hot summer afternoon. Time to play, ride bikes or hunt for lightning bugs.

The choice is one we all must make. Not to decide in favor of those we love is to choose against them. In the Sermon on the Mount, Jesus drew a picture of our present generation when he warned about becoming consumed with a quest for material things. "So do not worry, saying, 'What shall we eat?' or 'What shall we drink' or 'What shall we wear?' For the pagans *run* after all these things, and your Heavenly Father knows that you need them" (Matthew 6:31-32, italics ours).

The secret to spending more time with our spouses, our families, and those we love most is simple. Stop chasing after the wrong things. God knows our needs for living in this world. He's committed to taking care of us. We need to commit ourselves to loving those who need our love the most. If we make that choice, one of the most satisfying rewards will be time to "rejoice in the wife [or husband] of your youth."

Making time for children will be costly, but tremendously rewarding and extremely life-changing. The days you invest in your children spending time together will never be forgotten. The story is told of a father who kept a journal and once wrote, "Went fishing today—wasted the whole day." His son also happened to keep a diary and his entry for that day read, "Went fishing with my Dad today—it was the greatest day of my life." So to see the importance of giving up materialistic or career advances in favor of spending time with our children, we need to stop and look at life from their perspective for a moment.

How can you carve out not quality but quantity time? Put your kids into your calendar just behind time with your spouse. Consider teaching a class at their age level. Volunteer to lead a camping trip with their friends and their parents. Home-school them. Take them to the library one night every week. Buy a year-round swimming pass in your community. Bike together regularly. Go to a Christian family camp together.

Husbands, this intentional investment in your children will also pay dividends with your wife. Don't forget, researchers know that wives count the time the husbands spend with the kids as time spent with them—it's a double bonus.

2. Choose to give up what you can't keep to gain what you can't lose.

Those words are not our own. Rather, they are from the journal of Jim Elliott, a young man who died in Ecuador at the age of twenty-seven, trying to reach a primitive tribe with the love of Christ. Those words have profound meaning for a couple wanting to make time for the things that matter most.

Not far from our former home stood the Cuneo mansion. Once the luxurious estate of one of the wealthiest men in the Chicago area, it is now a museum. In other words, it's empty. You can eat brunch there on Sundays, and you can drive through the grounds at Christmastime to see a beautiful display of lights, and in the summer a local orchestra holds a series of concerts on its lawn. Otherwise the place is deserted except for the small security and maintenance staff.

When Mr. Cuneo was alive, it would have been hard for him to believe that everything he was working for would someday come down to a Christmas light show, Sunday brunch, or a performance of the *1812 Overture* on the Fourth of July. But that's what happened. Today, developers have bulldozed much of wooded property and built hundreds of tract homes.

We contrast that story with the story of a quiet, soft-spoken college professor named James "Buck" Hatch. On his eightieth birthday his son wrote a tribute to him, which read in part: "My parents' relationship as been a model of gentleness and respect. Dad didn't wait around to be waited upon. From bathing the children to washing the dishes, he did whatever would be of most help to my mother....Their commitment to a common ministry cemented their beautiful relationship....He has naturally gravitated to 'little' people, the ungifted, the unattractive, those often regarded as unlovely, or troublesome, or unuseful. As one deeply wounded person whom he couseled for years wrote, 'You have been Jesus in flesh and bone to me."[1] It was this man's love for his wife, their obvious loving and intimate marriage, and their time for others that impacted their son four decades later. That legacy can't be bulldozed or rezoned like an empty mansion; its influence will go on and on and on.

In order for us to build deeply satisfying and enriching relationships, we need time. But it will mean saying no to many things in order for us to say yes to what really matters.

"No, I'm afraid I can't come in this weekend to work. My wife and I are going away on a getaway this weekend."

"No, I don't think we'll buy a new car this year. Our budget won't allow it. Besides, there's a ministry in the inner city we intend to support."

"No, little Sweethearts, we can't drive you across town to attend a 9th birthday party this Saturday morning. It's our day together as a family."

Jesus asked a profound question: "What good will it be for a man if he gains the whole world, yet forfeits his soul?" (Matthew 16:26). How different from the businessman I recently read about. He said his family couldn't live with his demanding schedule at work. His solution? "I decided to get myself another family."

Your marriage is of great value in the eyes of God. Jesus made a remarkable statement in Matthew 19, verse 6: "Therefore what God has joined together, let man not separate." He claims our relationship with our spouse is more than just a legal agreement or a romantic partnership; it is a unique work of God. While marriage won't exist in heaven, the impact of the love and devotion we have shown to one another on earth will. It is worth making whatever sacrifices are necessary to nurture this valuable relationship.

3. Choose to put your spouse at the top of your priorities, second only to Christ.

We do have time for what we want to have time for. It's not that we don't have time to be with our spouse; it's that they aren't a high enough priority to us.

Imagine if we gave spending time with our spouses the same priority as eating, surfing the Net, or watching our favorite shows? What if we planned our time alone each evening as carefully as arriving at work on time? What if engaging in sex on a regular basis with our spouse was as important as going to the gym?

While it's possible for a couple to become too selfish of their time together, we rarely see that happening. What we see much more often is that marriage building is put on the waiting list, like buying siding for the garage to repair next year.

How can you make developing an intimate and fulfilling relationship with your spouse a top priority?

- Schedule time to be alone together every day, particularly to pray.

- Refuse all interruptions to your private time except emergencies.

- Budget and plan for regular and inexpensive dates.

- Choose activities (such as walking or biking) that both of you enjoy and can participate on a daily basis.

- Never accept a new obligation or time responsibility without consulting your spouse.

- Make marriage enrichment conferences a yearly part of your calendar.

- Discipline yourselves to turn off the television and go to bed early.

While there are more options than this, the principle is to make choices which create time for the two of you.

CONCLUSION

A rock group in the sixties coined the hit lyrics "Time won't let me...no, no." The truth is—time will let you. We have more hours and more control over those hours than we ever imagined.

Time will let us. The question is do we want to be together?

Chapter Ten

SEXUAL MAGNETISM IN MARRIAGE

THE COMMERCIALS FOR DESIGNER exotic fragrances and colognes are all pretty much the same. A man splashes on his musk-scented aftershave, walks out into public, and gorgeous models suddenly appear from every direction with desire burning in their eyes. A woman uses an expensive New York perfume, and suddenly she's transported to a Greek isle where rugged and attractive men follow her down the beach.

What the purveyors of modern scents are doing is as old as romance itself. They're trying to sell you and me on the notion that their product can instantly create sexual desire in another person. They hope to convince us they've discovered a modern aphrodisiac.

LEAH'S LOVE POTION

Is there such a thing as a love potion? Throughout history cultures have believed that certain plants or foods could heighten and intensify sexual passion, making a person irresistible to others. Believe it or not, that was even the case in the days of Jacob and Leah. After several years of being married to her reluctant husband, Leah pursued a desperate strategy to gain Jacob's love and affection. Anyone who accuses the Scriptures of lacking candor in describing human sexuality needs to re-read this story:

> During the wheat harvest, Reuben [Jacob and Leah's oldest son] went out into the fields and found some mandrake plants, which he brought to his mother Leah. Rachel said to Leah, "Please give me some of your son's mandrakes."
>
> But she said to her, "Wasn't it enough that you took away my husband? Will you take my son's mandrakes too?"

"Very well," Rachel said, "he can sleep with you tonight in return for your son's mandrakes."

So when Jacob came in from the fields that evening, Leah went out to meet him. "You must sleep with me," she said. "I have hired you with my son's mandrakes." So he slept with her that night.[1]

The story illustrates the pain and heartache that a troubled sex life can bring to marriage. It was perhaps common knowledge that Jacob and Leah's marriage was hurting. The fact that it had been years since the birth of her last child was a clue. Since Jacob's only interests in Leah appeared to be her ability to bear children, and since she had been infertile, we may assume Jacob now stayed away from her entirely.

Reuben was out in the fields during the harvest season when he discovered mandrakes growing in the wild. According to scholars, in ancient cultures mandrakes were believed to be aphrodisiacs and were highly prized (for obvious reasons).

Reuben ran home to show his mother his precious find. While it's a matter of pure speculation, he might have said something like, "Mother, look what I've found. Mandrakes. Please take them." Respect probably kept him from saying the obvious, but in his heart he must have been thinking, "These ought to get Dad interested in you again."

Word of Reuben's exotic find apparently spread quickly through the camp. Rachel, perhaps alarmed by the implication of Leah's possessing the mysterious love plant, rushed over and begged for a few samples of the love plant for herself.

The true state of Jacob and Leah's nonexistent sexual relationship is now confirmed. Listen to the pain in Leah's voice, "Wasn't it enough that you took away my husband? Will you take my son's mandrakes too?" A paraphrase of Leah's words might be, "Rachel, isn't it enough that Jacob sleeps only with you? Do you know how many nights I've watched him enter your tent while he walked past mine? Now that I've found something to offer me the slim hope that he might make love to me again and I might bear him another child, you want to steal that from me, too? Have you no shame, Rachel?"

Rachel, perhaps convicted by the truth of Leah's words or perhaps sensing she had lost control of the situation, decided to strike a bargain. She didn't want to leave the mandrakes in Leah's hands, fearing they might effectively arouse Jacob's passion and allow Leah to steal him away from her. So Rachel proposed a compromise. If Leah would turn over the mandrakes, she could have Jacob for one night.

Maybe Rachel was thinking, "What's only one night? Besides, after tonight, I'll be the one with the mandrakes, and Jacob won't be able to stay away from me."

If there is any lingering doubt about Jacob and Leah's sex life, listen to their discussion in the field. Jacob was returning from the day's work, tired and exhausted, when Leah ran out to meet him. She informed the surprised Jacob that she had purchased him for a one-night stand. "'You must sleep with me,' she said. 'I have hired you with my son's mandrakes.' So he slept with her that night." Jacob offered no protest over the deal, perhaps aroused by the news that Rachel had the love plant in her possession.

Can you imagine a marriage that has deteriorated to the point where one spouse has to hire the other for the night? That's exactly where Leah stood with Jacob.

Unfortunately, in many marriages that have gotten off-track, one partner couldn't even pay the other to make love. Oh, they may go through the act every once in a while, but without genuine tenderness or desire. It's more a duty or a matter of routine than an act of true marriage. As in the case of Leah, one partner becomes desperate to win back the affection and passion of the other.

ARTIFICIAL APHRODISIACS

While it's doubtful that mandrakes were actual aphrodisiacs, partners in unhappy marriages often are willing to try any artificial means to capture the sexual attention of their disinterested partner.

Sex on Paper

The most common form of a mandrake today is pornography. Couples will turn to Internet porn, magazines, R-rated or NC-17 videos, or other hard-core materials to arouse passion in their marriage. We're stunned by the number of couples who admit to allowing their partner to use pornographic magazines or literature during sexual intercourse to increase the sizzle in their love life. Its negative impact on people's attitudes toward marriage is well documented.[2] It's a great error for several reasons.

First, it won't lead to a sustained love life. Pornography is an addictive habit of diminishing returns. It requires greater and greater doses to achieve the same result, which means that using pictures and videos to turn on your partner will eventually give out. It can't sustain the high.

We remember an advertisement in a popular news magazine that showed a couple sitting in front of a television, holding shot glasses of whisky and watching a sexy video. It was intended to titillate the consumer into believing that Jack Daniels and erotic movies combine to create the ultimate lovemaking experience. The truth is, it may work at first. But over time more bottles of liquor and sexier videos are required to achieve the same effect.

Which leads to the second problem. Inevitably, the use of pornography in lovemaking leads to more sordid and aberrant materials. As the graphic nature of the pornographic literature increases, it becomes more bizarre and abnormal, drawing couples further away from normal sexual activity.

Finally, the use of pornography in the bedroom or on the Internet is essentially sex with someone else. At best, it's sexual fantasizing about another person. At worst, it's visual adultery. It feeds lust for a person you've never met, desire for an individual you'll never have a genuine relationship with, and hunger for someone you have no commitment to, or they to you. It's sex in Cyberspace or a DVD.

The bonding process is intended to progress between two real human beings who actually see, talk to, and touch each other. Sex with the aid of pornography, whether magazines or Internet, transfers that highly intense emotional and psychological attachment to someone other than your spouse. The result is a distancing and detachment from your own life's partner. It's as if you're making love to two different people at the same time. You've allowed another lover to enter the bedroom. That's as destructive to true intimacy as anything we can think of.

Perhaps the most famous article in the history of *Leadership Journal* was a minister's account of his private struggle with lust. He admitted that he started down the road toward pornography addiction the weekend he visited a bar with nude dancers. For the next several years his life was a nightmare of increasingly compulsive and obsessive behaviors that nearly destroyed his marriage and career.

In desperation, he sought the counsel of an older and respected pastor. As he poured out his secret pain, the older pastor stared at him, then began blinking back tears, and eventually broke into sobs. The older pastor handed the younger one several prescriptions he was taking to treat his own STD's. The older minister confessed to decades of immoral behavior, which began with using pornography earlier in his life. It had cost him everything worthwhile.

Fortunately, the story has a redemptive ending. The younger pastor was so frightened by the prospect of ending up like the older pastor that he resolved to find help and give up his addiction. The article ends with the pastor sharing that once he found freedom from his habit his marriage changed dramatically. His sexual relationship with his wife took on a new beauty and meaning he had never known. He felt purity and love energize their relationship, rather than the insatiable and demanding obsession that pornography had created in his life.[3]

Getting High

Drugs and alcohol are two other artificial aphrodisiacs that some couples use to try to stimulate a disappointing love life. The myth is that sex is best while you're drunk or high. But it's just that—a myth.

If a couple is resorting to chemical substances in order to enjoy each other, the clock is already ticking on the eventual destruction of their relationship. Drugs can no more build intimacy or satisfaction in a relationship than they can help any of us face life's problems more effectively. They may anesthetize our emotional pain, or allow us a few minutes of relief from our inhibitions, but overall the addictive nature of drugs ensures that they will steal more happiness from us than they will ever be able to offer. Just ask the husband and wife of an alcoholic how much better booze makes their sex life. Bob's counseling experience suggests that many men who are alcoholics struggle with impotency. Sobriety is their only hope for regaining the ability to be intimate with their wives. Ephesians 5:18 says, "Do not get drunk on wine, which leads to debauchery. Instead, be filled with the Spirit."

Sexual happiness in marriage can't be purchased on EBay, rolled and smoked behind closed doors, or bought in the back room of an adult bookstore. These "aphrodisiacs" miss the point of true sexual intimacy, because it really is a matter of the heart.

THE TRUE APHRODISIACS

Here's the good news. Young or old, rich or poor, handsome or homely, every married individual can possess the true love stimulants of marriage.

What are these mysterious formulas for heightened and sustaining sexual enjoyment in marriage? They may surprise you. They are *forgiveness, surrender, unselfishness, and respect.* More than anything else we know, they can restore pleasure and fulfillment to a couple's sex life. They are the true aphrodisiacs, found not in mysterious plants or rain forests, but in the souls of a man and woman. Generous doses of each one, taken regularly, can rejuvenate a sexual relationship.

The Magnetism of Forgiveness

Forgiveness—an aphrodisiac that's available in all parts of the world, but rarely used. When it is used, it can dramatically alter the chemistry between two people. As we discussed in the last chapter, the negative emotions of anger and fear can destroy the sexual relationship between a husband and wife. If we're seething with bitterness toward our mate, there's little or no chance we'll seek out or accept sexual intimacy.

We watched a talk show one afternoon that featured couples who had decided to get a divorce. When one husband was asked if it bothered him that his estranged wife had taken a lover, he replied, "I don't care what she does. In fact, I hope she's run over by a train one of these days. That way I can get her out of my life." Imagine, he wanted her dead.

But if anger can drive a couple that far apart, forgiveness can have just the opposite effect. It can be positively magnetic. Think back on the worst fights you and your spouse have ever had. Were you able to resolve those arguments, perhaps with tears, by offering and receiving genuine forgiveness? Do you remember where that led? Chances are, you soon were enjoying the best sex you had experienced in a long time. The old adage is true, "The best part of fighting is making up."

Why this sudden burst of sexual attraction when a couple resolves a fight? It's simple. Once our essential oneness has been restored, we want to express that in a physical way. A depth of intimacy has just been achieved. We feel more understood, more appreciated, more accepted for who we are, and that ignites the main engines of sexual desire and fuels passion with white hot intensity.

But giving forgiveness is not always easy. How do we forgive a person we don't feel like forgiving? Or someone who hasn't even asked for our forgiveness? It's not easy, we'll grant you. If it were, more couples would choose that route rather than divorce court.

As Neil Anderson points out, forgiveness is essentially a choice we make, not a feeling we achieve. It requires, by an act of our will, releasing other people from the moral debt they owe us. Forgiveness is not given because it's earned or deserved, but because it's needed. Forgiveness is mercy, not justice.

The story is told of a soldier during the Revolutionary War who had deserted the ranks and was later captured. He was tried and sentenced to die. The order was about to be carried out when a Methodist circuit-riding preacher by the name of Peter Miller rode breathless into the camp.

"I must see General Washington," he said. He was ushered into the general's tent. There he explained that he had ridden for an entire day to ask for a pardon for the condemned soldier.

"Is he a friend of yours?" Washington asked?

"No, he is one of my worst enemies," the preacher replied, still breathing hard.

"You rode for an entire day to ask for a pardon for your worst enemy? Why?"

"Because he needs it," Miller replied.

Washington was so moved by Miller's act of grace that he granted the pardon. That's precisely the point of forgiveness. We offer it because it's needed, not because it's deserved.

What makes forgiveness difficult is our innate desire for justice. Something within us demands that punishment be paid for a wrong we've experienced.

"I will forgive my wife when she finally admits she's been wrong all these years."

"I won't forgive Brandon until he quits making thoughtless remarks about me."

"He can't just say 'I'm sorry' and think that makes everything all right."

If necessary, we can dredge up enough from the past to justify a lifetime of grudges. We can rationalize a thousand and one reasons to be vindictive. And if we refuse to forgive until the other person has paid his debt to us, when is the payment sufficient? When has the other person suffered enough? How much pain does he or she actually deserve? Do we know just the right amount?

If we don't offer forgiveness, then we become lifetime prisoners of our making. We stay bound by our own bitterness, acrimony, and resentment.

After the Civil War had ended, General Robert E. Lee was visiting in the home of a woman whose property had been pillaged by the invading Union army. A once beautiful oak tree now stood gnarled and disfigured on the front yard.

"What should I do, General?" the woman asked, her face etched with anger and her voice brimming with revenge.

"Madam, I would cut it down and forget about it," he calmly replied. The

General had learned not only to command armies but his emotions as well – often a far more difficult task.

Forgiveness occurs when we choose to override our desire for punishment and payment and we release our husband or wife from any further moral debt to us. It may come with difficulty, it may come slowly, it may even come in stages, but if it is our desire to forgive, it will occur.

The resources of God can be of such help here. He is by nature forgiving, and He offers us the strength and ability to forgive our mate when everything within us screams, "No! No! I can never forgive what has been done to me." Even couples who have endured the nightmare of adultery, or who have discovered painful things about each other's past, have found that forgiveness can heal their relationship. The memories, the hurt, and the scars may endure, but forgiveness allows the marriage to go forward.

After they were married, Abdul learned that Anita had been intimate with other men when she was single. It took months of dealing with his anger, hurt, and disappointment before he could show affection toward her again. Part of him wanted to forgive her; the other part wanted to punish her for her earlier immorality. Eventually Abdul realized that Anita could not change her past, even if she wanted to. The only thing that could be changed was his attitude toward her past. He decided to focus on his love for her and her faithfulness to him throughout their married life. His willingness to forgive rekindled the intimacy in their marriage, allowing them both to go on with their lives and leave the past behind. What a shame if a lack of forgiveness had been allowed to destroy a truly beautiful relationship.

The Triumph of Surrender

Surrender is the second white-hot emotional aphrodisiac that can enhance a couple's sex life.

All of us bring fears, inhibitions, and insecurities to our marriage, which will eventually surface in our sexual relationship. The level of intimacy and vulnerability that the Creator designed into the sex act forces these hidden fears to come out.

Olivia was raised in an emotionally distant home. Her parents insisted that she be perfect at everything she did, and with a sweet face and natural talents, she seemed to meet their every expectation. But over time her view of love became distorted. She believed that her parents' love and acceptance were based on her being the perfect daughter. Part of that perfect daughter image was shaped by the subtle message that sex was dirty and nice girls should have no interest in it. Olivia confused the truth that sex outside of marriage is wrong with the idea that her sexual person itself was wrong.

To her credit, she remained a virgin throughout her teenage years and into young adulthood. After college she met a solid guy whom she fell in love with and planned to marry. Little did Olivia know it, but she was headed for real problems in her relationship with her husband. Years of associating acceptance and love with a denial of her own sexuality set her up for a train-wreck.

It happened on the honeymoon. When she and her new husband reached the bridal suite, she broke out in hives. In her mind, engaging in sexual intercourse would completely destroy her perfect daughter image, the basis for her self-acceptance growing up. Sexual intercourse would sully her, leaving her a "less than perfect" person, or so her distorted conscience told her.

She wanted to be intimate with her husband, but she couldn't get past the feeling she was doing something wrong. Her feelings that sex was disgusting, even dirty, were simply overwhelming, and her skin betrayed the anguish inside.

But an understanding of surrender in marriage can heal even someone like Olivia. God never designed anything that was disgusting, dirty, or sinful. Sexuality is among his highest gifts to humanity. In the context of marriage the sexual act is pure, life giving, even holy in His sight. But it requires surrender in order to be enjoyed to its fullest.

What is surrender in marriage? It's essentially giving our life away in order to get it back again. It is in no sense giving up our right to be an individual, or becoming the slave of another, or eradicating our personhood, dignity, or uniqueness. Surrender is voluntarily yielding ourselves to another in love. It is letting go of the fears and inhibitions that create barriers between two people whom God designed to "become one flesh."

Let's suppose a building is on fire. On the third floor balcony a terrified tenant hangs on to the railing with a death grip. As a brave fireman climbs the ladder and reaches him, he urges the man to let go of the railing so he may be carried to safety. The flames are roaring, smoke is billowing, and the person is scared to death. He can choose either to hang on and lose his life, or let go and get it back again. That's surrender. In the same fashion, when we let go of our fears and apprehensions and choose to trust another human being in the act of sexual intimacy, we haven't lost who we are. We've surrendered ourselves to our partner's love and care and have found a new dimension of human happiness.

That's the paradox of life. When we give up, we gain back. When we yield, we overcome. When we sacrifice, we are enriched.

Real surrender in marriage is not one-sided. A biblical view of sex calls for mutual submission. Remember the apostle's words: "The wife's body does not belong to her alone but also to her husband. In the same way, the husband's body does not belong to him alone but also to his wife."[4] The apostle says surrender is reciprocal, mutual, two-sided.

Olivia had the mistaken notion that she had lost something when she engaged in intercourse with her husband. Not at all. In surrendering her body to her husband, and he doing likewise, they both gained the union and "one flesh" that the Creator designed to give us maximum fulfillment and joy in marriage.

What Olivia needed to lose was her false sense of guilt and shame. Her upbringing of perfectionism and conditional love had left her feeling sinful for enjoying the intimacy God designed for marriage. She needed to surrender her false ideas that her sexuality was a curse, not a blessing. She also needed to realize that God values us, not because we earn it, but because He loves us just as we are.

The Dividends of Unselfishness

The third steaming aphrodisiac—and perhaps the most elusive—is unselfishness.

The popular euphamism for sexual intercourse is "making love." Although we, too, use this expression, we've always been somewhat baffled by the term. How do you "make" something that can only be given?

Making love sounds too much like the mere mechanical joining of a male and female body. Giving love sounds much more like the sharing of your soul, your affection, your respect, your deepest concern, and your heart with another person.

All too often when it comes to sex, we are out to get something, not give something. The result may be passionate and frenzied lovemaking for a season, but the inevitable result of emphasizing getting rather than giving is disappointment, loss of interest, and finally frustration.

Imagine applying the following definitions of "giving love" to your sexual relationship: "Love is patient, love is kind. It does not envy, it does not boast, it is not proud. It is not rude, it is not self-seeking, it is not easily angered, it keeps no record of wrongs. Love does not delight in evil but rejoices with the truth. It always protects, always trusts, always hopes, always perseveres"

(I Corinthians 13:4-7). That type of "giving love" will improve and enhance the quality of your love life in ways that will be hard to imagine.

Men can easily become self-centered, particularly when it comes to sexuality. The nature of a male's sexual functioning predisposes us to quick arousal and quick satisfaction. Women, on the other hand, sometimes take far longer to become sexually excited and usually take longer to be satisfied. It's the difference between a dragster and a freight train. Dragster cars roar to life, squeal off the starting line, and, before you know it, put on the brakes. Freight trains, on the other hand, take a long time to get rolling. But once they do, they're hard to stop.

If wives have one persistent complaint about their husbands' sexual performance, it is that they rush things. Husbands become so preoccupied with satisfying their own needs, due to their quick arousal, they forget to bring their mate along with them. While it may be natural for men, it is also quite selfish.

"As soon as my husband is finished, he goes to sleep" is a common complaint among women. It's a clear signal that the husband has not taken time to arouse his wife with physical and emotional foreplay, nor stayed around to ensure that she has experienced climax as well. Good sex begins with taking care of our mate's needs, not our own. We should not deny each other a sexual relationship, or act bored or disinterested in the middle of making love.

I (Bob) once counseled a couple, both recovering alcoholics, who were having serious marriage problems. When I had a chance to sit down with them, the wife began ridiculing her husband's sexual performance. "I can't tell you how many times it's ended just as soon as it got started," she said as she lit a cigarette. "He says, 'woops' and it's all over." She blew smoke in his direction. I saw him slink down in his chair, humiliated. What she said may have been true, but her sarcastic smirk sent the loud and clear message she considered him a failure. I suspected the real problem in their sexual relationship was not his premature ejaculations, but her predominant disrespect for him. The two were probably related.

Some experts suggest women experience their sexual arousal more on a psycho-social-physiological level. It is the tenderness and communication in the relationship that excite women. Perhaps the best technique for helping a woman achieve climax in the sexual act is to show her tenderness, talk to her, and stimulate her mind and imagination. That's why love, sensitivity, and romance are so important to meeting the sexual needs of a woman.

Women buy more romance novels than men do. It's not because they contain steamy and prurient scenes (although many do), but because they focus on romance and relationships. That's a deeply felt need in the female soul. Husbands who fail to romance their wives throughout the day often find a disinterested or disappointed mate awaiting them when they finally slip into bed at night. It's a little late at 11:30 p.m. to start showing a real interest in communication and tenderness when you ignored her at 5:00 p.m. (although it's worth a try).

Men, on the other hand, operate far more on a visual, biological and less emotional level. Simply seeing a woman is enough to provide sexual arousal (all the fashion designers understand this). Whether or not a word is exchanged all day between the two, the husband can be ready for action at a moment's notice.

Unselfishness can help restore passion to a couple's love life. As spouses, we must listen to each other, talk together, and show one another sensitivity and tenderness. We must communicate to our mates that they are attractive and important to us.

Once we move into the bedroom, we need to take things slow. We need to hug and hold our spouse in a caring and intimate manner, not simply for sexual stimulation. Fortunately, it doesn't have to be an either/or choice. We need to take the time to say, "You are cherished and loved."

I (Bob) still recall as a young man sitting in the office of my pastor one day when his wife pulled up in front of the church. "Excuse me, Bob," he said. "I must go make love to my wife." Single at the time, I was left speechless as he disappeared out the door and hopped into the front seat of his wife's car. He did go make love to her, but not in the popular sense of the term. For nearly thirty minutes he sat hugging her and cuddling her. I stood at the window, shaking my head in disbelief at a married couple being so affectionate in public.

He taught me a valuable lesson that day: Making love to your wife begins long before you close the bedroom door.

Husbands need to take the time to ensure their wives experience sexual release and fulfillment. Far too many men simply turn over and start snoring once they've been satisfied. That's selfishness in its purest sense. Women are capable of achieving multiple climaxes during intercourse. It's the sensitive and giving husband who makes sure her needs are satisfied before his.

If you have specific questions in this area, we suggest you discuss the matter with a counselor or your personal physician. He or she can help explain the proper methods of ensuring both partners experience the joy and pleasure God designed into this sacred, mysterious, and bonding experience. There are numerous helpful books on the subject as well, such as *Sheet Music* by Dr. Kevin Leman or *The Celebration of Sex* by Dr. Douglas Rosenau.

Unselfishness which builds intimacy should extend beyond the bedroom. It ought to be a way of life. We suggest couples do three things each day, even if they don't feel like it.

First, hug each other for at least ninety seconds. It may feel awkward at first, but the payoffs are enormous. Real and important transactions take place in a relationship when we hold each other in our arms for an extended period of time.

Second, we suggest couples call one another at least twice during the day. It allows you to stay in touch, to remain connected, so that all your distracting business doesn't have to be handled when you get home at night.

Finally, we suggest you ask each other, "What do you need from me at this very moment?" That type of unselfish question can do much to help a burdened or overworked person find love and comfort in a relationship. When our spouses need time alone, we need to gather up the kids and offer them the gift of silence and tranquility. When our mates need someone to talk to, we need to put down remote, look them in the eye, and listen. When they just need to be held, we need to enfold them and assure them of how much we love them.

All of these unselfish acts are cumulative in a marriage. Over time they actually cause us to love our spouse more. The more unselfishly we treat someone, the more highly we value them. The more highly we value them, the more we love them. It's a delicious—not vicious—cycle that leads upward.

The Value of Respect

An added final powerful come-on is to show our spouse respect, particularly wives to their husbands. We all crave respect and admiration, and they ignite passion. On the other hand, one of the best ways to destroy sexual interest is to show disrespect for our mate.

"If I don't keep reminding Roger to speak up at gatherings, he'll never make any friends."

"Kim, that's an ugly blouse. You need to ask me before you wear something like that."

"David, when are you going to fix this sink? This is the fourth time I've had to ask you. Other husbands take care of things like this without ever having to be asked."

Remember the poll of the four hundred divorced men? Their number one criterion for their next mate was someone who treated them as if they were "best friends." Best friends don't put each other down in public, share embarrassing facts about each other on the telephone, or criticize each other at home.

Funny thing about respect. The more we offer it to someone, the more we enjoy being with that person. The less respect we show, the less often we care to spend time together.

None of us should dare to assume the role of re-Creator in someone else's life. If God made some people quiet, shy, and reflective, we have no business trying to turn them into extroverts who enjoy wearing loud shirts and working as a greeter at a Disney store. If God made others artsy, creative, and spontaneous, it's pure presumption to try to transform them into technical, detail-oriented, accountants.

Nine times out of ten we try to remake spouses in our own image. That's a mistake. To begin with, we're flawed goods, too. If they don't have the same temperament, emotional makeup, and talents we do, it's futile to spend years trying to reshape their basic personality structure. We might make them nervous and miserable, but we'll never change who they truly are.

The truth is we don't have to be exactly alike to love and respect each other. Nor is it our personal responsibility to spend a lifetime re-tooling my mate. Our time and energy would be much better spent reworking who we are so that we will get along better with that person.

A Word about Trust

To establish a healthy sex life requires an enormous amount of trust between two people. That trust includes a commitment to utter faithfulness. Some researchers have suggested that women can only experience climax to the extent they have complete trust in their husbands. Trust is not simply a luxury or option in experiencing true sexual fulfillment; it's mandatory.

Let us suggest some steps we can take to build trust with our spouses:

1. *Maintain the privacy of your sexual relationship.* Don't discuss the intimate details of your sex life with relatives, friends, or co-workers. Of course, if you're having problems and need professional advice, never hesitate to seek out a Christian counselor or pastor. But no one else needs to know how often you make love or what's said and done behind closed doors. That's your business. An important element of your bond is the secrets known only to the two of you.

2. *Contact each other frequently when you're apart.* In a time when people often travel or work long hours, it's important to stay in close contact with each other. It helps prevent temptation and at the same time promotes intimacy. Simple phone calls in the morning and evening when on the road, or perhaps some conversations during breaks at work, help cement trust. We're not keeping tabs on each other; we're staying connected.

3. *Compliment each other the morning after.* We can't stress enough how important it is to affirm each other as lovers—not just before you both drift off to sleep but the next morning too. In fact, in discreet ways we should be consistently complimenting our spouse's body and lovemaking skills and the enjoyment we experience from being with him or her. Compliments the morning after build up self-esteem and trust. They also place our sexual relationship in the broader context of our everyday life together.

4. *Talk to each other.* As intimate as the sexual relationship can be, it also holds the potential to be quite lonely and anonymous at times. It is far more than a physical act; it is the mysteious process of two becoming one.

That requires sharing our feelings and communicating our thoughts with each other. More than one therapist has suggested the value of looking into one another's eyes and communicating with each other during sexual intimacy. Achieving orgasm is not the primary goal; expressing love and intimacy is. Climax should be a by-product, not an end within itself. There is a bonding in the sexual act that transcends explanation, a uniting of souls as well as bodies. In warning against sexual sin Paul made a profound observation about the mystery of sex: "Do you not know that he who unites himself with a prostitute is one with her in body? For it is said, 'The two shall become one flesh'" (I Corinthians 6:16). It is through our eyes that an element of that "oneness" is experienced.

Husbands, learn to share verbally with your wife how much they mean to you. Tell them how much you love them. Assure them you treasure and cherish them. Tell them how attractive and beautiful you find them. Be specific on characteristics of her body that you enjoy—if you need an example of this, read Song of Solomon. Those compliments and assurances will bring a dimension of fulfillment and intimacy to the sexual experience for your wife that defies description.

Wives, tell your husband you love and admire them. Tell them how thrilled you are to be sharing this experience with them. Compliment them on their strength and body. Helping your husbands feel respected and admired brings a dimension of fulfillment and intimacy to their sexual experience. Response from you to your husband's loving is an essential element of male sexual fulfillment.

It really goes back to the basic advice Paul gave husbands and wives in Ephesians: "However, each of you also must love his wife as he loves himself, and the wife must respect her husband" (5:33). That simple formula can transform a dull or disappointing sexual relationship into a high voltage and fulfilling love life.

For Appearance' Sake

One final word of caution to wives and husbands both. Don't let go of your appearance simply because you're married and the courting game is over. Men simply want their wives to still look as if they are meeting someone important—their husbands. Wives aren't expecting Brad Pitt or George Clooney look-alikes either, but they do appreciate men who watch their weight and keep themselves in good shape.

Of course, age will eventually change the bodies of both men and women. And when we're bald, stooped over, or gray, the deeper work of love and respect will pay its dividends. We will still feel attractive for each other, not based on outward appearances but on the bonding that has occurred in our souls.

One of our dear friends was a lady ninety-two years old. She and her husband were married over fifty years. They survived both world wars, the Depression, the Cold War, and all the other tumultuous events of the 20th century before he died at that age of eighty-six. Up to the end her husband's picture still hung in her bedroom, and when she spoke of him, the respect in her voice conveyed that she truly loved him. His last picture shows a tired man with drawn eyes. But to her, he left this world the most attractive man she had ever met—and now they are together again in heaven.

CONCLUSION

Obsession. Victoria's Secret. Musk. You've heard the names and seen the commercials. They are the modern mandrakes, the aphrodisiacs that promise compulsive attraction between the sexes. But in the end, they are just a seventy-five-dollar-an-ounce disappointment. The human personality structure is simply too complicated to be controlled by exotic fragrances or lingerie. True sexual attraction and fulfillment in marriage are the result of our character, not our cologne. Forgiveness, surrender, unselfishness and respect—when offered in love and sincerity—are the elements of irresistible love.

PART
THREE

Chapter Eleven

THE HIGHER AND HIDDEN PURPOSES OF GOD

THE LATE TRUMAN ROBERTSON, a good friend of ours, was the founder and director of Fort Wilderness, a beautiful camp in the north woods of Wisconsin. One summer day he asked two young boys to go burn the camp garbage. The two eager campers readily agreed and headed off to the garbage pit. Once they got there, they hit on an ingenious plan to take care of the job faster and more efficiently.

They found a five-gallon container of high-octane gasoline and decided to soak the garbage before lighting the match. They were about to set the rubbish ablaze when they decided it might be wise to put a little distance between the bonfire and themselves.

Then they hit upon another stroke of genius. They took a bow and arrow, tied a rag on the end of the arrow, and lit it just as they had seen in a Western movie. Taking careful aim, they let it fly. The projectile followed a perfect arc into the center of the pit.

The ensuing explosion was heard for several miles. Onlookers claim to have seen soup cans, corncobs, and milk cartons fly at least fifty feet into the sky. Garbage literally rained down on the camp like leftovers from heaven.

The two boys, hunched down behind a rock, were nearly deafened by the blast. When they cautiously emerged to survey the devastation, they were speechless. Garbage dangling from the trees. Debris was scattered in every direction. All that was left of the garbage was a crater approximately twenty feet deep.

It had all seemed like such a good idea. But the best that could be said was that no one had been killed.

The same is true of many marriages. They start out as such a good idea. The engagement, the wedding, the new life together. But when the marital explosions hit and people are left dazed, covered with emotional debris, and staring into a gaping pit of despair and unhappiness, they are tempted to stop and ask, "Was this all a big mistake?"

Every time we meet people who are going through a divorce, or who have fallen into adultery, or who simply hate being married, we're reminded that they didn't have this in mind that beautiful Saturday afternoon in June. As they dressed in elegant clothes and recited solemn vows, surrounded by friends and family, they never dreamed it would turn out like this. They now think, "I wasn't supposed to hate her as much as I do." "I wasn't supposed to get this sick feeling in my stomach when I hear him come home at night." "I wasn't supposed to end up dreading each family get-together where I have to pretend everything is all right when it isn't."

When people reach the conclusion that their marriage never should have been, the next logical question is "Then why go on? It's stupid. This obviously wasn't the right thing to do, so why don't I just end it?"

BUT WHAT DOES GOD THINK?

That's where we would like to interrupt their train of thought and challenge them with this question, "Who says that it's all a big mistake?" On what authority can you or I announce that our marriage never should have been? Because our feelings tell us so? Or because our parents think our mate is a loser? Or because a counselor has told us we need to leave the marriage to find happiness and freedom? Before we pack our bags or call the lawyer, we need to consider this question: "Does God think my marriage was a big mistake?"

"What do you mean what does God think?" someone might protest. "How in the world am I supposed to know the mind of God anyway? All I know is that I'm terribly unhappy and a loving God could never want anyone to feel as bad as I do."

We agree that God doesn't enjoy seeing you suffer emotional pain and sorrow. His heart hurts when yours does. But that doesn't mean that your marriage is a big mistake. All it means is that you are unhappy and at the moment you feel your marriage is a big mistake.

ANYTHING OF VALUE
IS WORTH SUFFERING FOR

Let's imagine for a moment that you and us had an opportunity to talk about your marriage at a time when you were fed up and wanting out.

"Bob and Cheryl, my marriage is a disaster. It's the biggest regret of my life. I should have never married the person I did."

Our response might be, "We hear your pain, your unhappiness, and your desire to see something change in your marriage. But we're not convinced that your marriage is a big mistake."

"Why not? How could I be this unhappy and possibly be married to the right person?"

"Let us answer that with another question. Was going through college worthwhile?"

"Well, of course it was."

"Did you ever want to quite, particularly during finals weeks?"

"Sure. I got so tired and worn out I wanted to drop out and never look back. I hated school during those weeks."

"Let us ask you another question" (assuming we're now talking to a woman). "When you had your first child and you were in the midst of hard labor, did you ever wish you had not decided to get pregnant in the first place?"

"Are you kidding? Men will never understand just how painful having a baby can get."

"But was it worth the agony?"

"Of course. I love my daughter. I wouldn't trade her for anything in the world."

"Then can we agree that even though you endured great suffering, what you gained from the experience offset the sacrifice involved?"

"Yes."

"If you can accept that, then let us suggest the pain you're experiencing today is not iron-clad evidence you married the wrong person. Pain can only tell you something is wrong and needs to be addressed in your relationship. That's quite different from saying your marriage is a big mistake."

Ask people who have labored, fought, cried, hurt, but persevered in a worthwhile task, and they will tell you it's become a valuable, if not the most valuable, experience of their entire life. Sigmund Freud said, "Someday, given enough time, we will look back on our lives and discover the most difficult moments have become the most precious to us."

In the same way, it may seem pointless today to endure the pain and hardship of a marriage that started off wrong. And if we project our feeling out another five, ten, or fifty years, staying in the marriage seems too much to ask. No one can or should live with that much unhappiness we tell ourselves.

But just as the tumultuous times eventually pass, so a difficult season in a marriage can give way to a much more fulfilling and joyful experience. Ask a couple who has made it to the half-century mark, and they'll no doubt tell you about some grim years along the way—the time he lost his job, or one of their children died at birth, or a close family member was struck down with a disease. But if you watch closely, particularly the way they look into each other's eyes, you'll probably catch a glimpse of the deep understanding that exists between them. They will quietly acknowledge to each other, "We went through that together, and we survived it. I thank God that I had you to go through it with me."

Let us assure you, we're no advocate of masochism. We don't believe in suffering for the sake of suffering, nor should you gain any pleasure from it. But we do believe in the redemptive value of our pain if we use it to our advantage. If we make it serve us, if we allow it to do its good work in our lives, if we use it to motivate us to take action, then it can become something positive.

It all comes back to believing there is an authority higher than our emotions, our immediate circumstances, or the opinion of others. It goes back to believing that God may have a higher and unseen purpose in our marriage than we realize at the moment. Trusting that He is working out a plan for our lives can make all the difference.

LESSONS FROM LEAH

Let's go back to Jacob and Leah. Leah is, by our standards, a remarkable woman. If *Time* magazine had been in existence almost four thousand years ago, she would have been our nomination for Person of the Year.

If any woman on earth at the time had the right to say, "God? What God?" it was Leah. She had virtually no rights as a female member of an ancient tribal society. She was used by her father to cheat Jacob out of another seven years of free labor. Jacob hardly treated her as a wife. Yet she refused to surrender her faith that God was demonstrating his love and concern for her. That's evident from the names she gave her sons. Each one was an acknowledgement that God was quietly, if not mysteriously, involved in the events of her life.

When Reuben was born, she said, "*It is because the Lord has seen* my misery." When Simeon entered the world, she confessed, "*Because the Lord heard* that I am not loved, he gave me this one too." The same was true at the birth of Issachar: "*God has rewarded me.*" And Zebulun: "*God has presented me* with a precious gift."[1] When each of her six sons was born, Leah claimed it was proof that God had not forgotten her but was showering her with his mercy and affection.   Her faith continued in spite of the fact that Jacob kept treating her like a second-class citizen. Although Leah hoped that her sons would change his heart, there is little evidence that he softened toward her at this early stage in his life.   Nonetheless, Leah continued to believe and worship God.

Anyone who is struggling with a disappointing or "unbearable" marriage can take great encouragement from the example of Leah. Her life is proof that outward circumstances are not always an indication of God's concern and compassion for us. Just because our marriage is hurting doesn't mean God no longer loves us. He may be using this particularly agonizing period in our life to communicate with us.

The great Oxford scholar C.S. Lewis once wrote, "Pain is God's megaphone." It does get our attention. It does drive us from our self-sufficiency to seek the help and strength that God longs to offer us. Lewis wrote from his own experience. A confirmed bachelor for most of his life, he eventually married a woman who was suffering from cancer. By most accounts, he did it more out of duty than of love.

But in the few years they were married, he learned to love his wife, Joy, deeply. By the time she died, she had become the most precious person on earth to him. In his book *A Grief Observed* Lewis shares his heart-rending experience of losing the person he had learned to love more than his own life.

Which brings us back to Leah. The worse things were with Jacob, the more real God seemed to her. Was she in denial? Was her faith in God just a spiritual fix to get her through another tough week with a loveless husband and a jealous sister? Was the "God talk" just a crutch? Or was God truly the strength of her life?

The answer lies in the birth of her fourth son, Judah. In that event God honored Leah's confidence that He was working in her life in some mysterious and wonderful fashion. When Leah's fourth son was born, she said, "'This time I will praise the Lord.' So she named him Judah." Scholars note that the name Judah sounds like and is probably derived from the Hebrew word for "praise."[2]

You may still be asking, "But how does naming a child 'Judah' prove that Leah's faith was real? How does that prove God was working behind the scenes in her life and marriage to accomplish a higher and hidden purpose?"

LEAH IN THE PLAN OF GOD

That's where a bit of biblical history is useful. As far back as the Garden of Eden when Adam and Eve first rebelled against God, a promise was made by God himself that one day the "seed" of a woman would crush the head of the serpent (the personification of the devil).[3] In other words, God was promising that one day a child would be born who would destroy the dominion and work of the evil one in our world.

This promise was later passed on to Abraham when God pledged, "All peoples on earth will be blessed through you."[4] The blessing was to come through Abraham's son Isaac. When Isaac's son Jacob was just a young man, God appeared to him in a dream and said, "All the peoples on earth will be blessed through you and your offspring."[5] Later, Judah was born to Jacob and Leah.

Near the end of his life Jacob gathered all of his sons to his bedside and pronounced a blessing on them. When Judah knelt beside his elderly father, Jacob said, "You are a lion's cub, O Judah;...The scepter will not depart from Judah, nor the ruler's staff from between his feet, until he comes to whom it belongs, and the obedience of the nations is his."[6] Jacob was predicting that the royal leadership of the nation of Israel would be established through his son Judah, and God's promise to Abraham, Isaac, and Jacob would be fulfilled in him.

If we fast-forward the tape several hundred years, we discover that a young shepherd boy named David, a descendant of Jacob and Leah, was eventually chosen to be king over the entire nation. "Then the men of Judah came to Hebron and there they anointed David king over the house of Judah."[7] David, the greatest king in the history of Israel, a man who conquered giants, drove out foreign enemies, and established the nation as the greatest of its time, was the direct descendant of Jacob—and Leah.

Where is all this genealogy leading? And what does this have to do with Leah's faith in God?

Jump ahead to approximately 4 B.C., to a small village named Nazareth.

The gospel of Luke tells us:

> In the sixth month, God sent the angel Gabriel to Nazareth, a town in
> Galilee, to a virgin pledged to be married to a man named Joseph, a descendant
> of David. The virgin's name was Mary. The angel went to her and said,
> "Greeting, you who are highly favored! The Lord is with you."
>
> Mary was greatly troubled at his words and wondered what kind of
> greeting this might be. But the angel said to her, "Do not be afraid, Mary, you
> have found favor with God. You will be with child and give birth to a son,
> and you are to give him the name Jesus. He will be great and will be called
> the Son of the Most High. The Lord God will give him the throne of his
> father David, and he will reign over the *house of Jacob* forever; his kingdom
> will never end."[8]

Luke puts the final piece of the puzzle in place when he gives us the family
genealogy of Mary, the mother of Jesus. He traces her ancestry back through
her father, Heli. Heli was a descendant of "David, the son of Jesse...the son of
Judah, the *son of Jacob*, the son of Isaac, the son of Abraham...the son of
Adam, the son of God."[9]

There it is—the story of God's mysterious working in Leah's life. Although
she did not fully understand the role she was playing, she was being used by
God to complete a promise made to Adam, affirmed to Abraham, and then
passed on to Jacob, and from Jacob to Judah. Through Jacob and Leah's fourth
son, Judah, came David, Solomon, Joseph, Mary, and eventually Jesus, the Christ.
Even though Jacob may have loved Rachel more, it was through Leah that God
created the ancestral line that eventually gave us the Savior.

What if Leah had simply given up on her marriage? What if she had allowed
her feelings to dictate that she should leave Jacob to take another lover? God
literally used Leah's faith in His higher and hidden purposes for her marriage to
help accomplish the salvation of the world.

Back to the question we asked earlier: Was Leah right to believe that God
was working in her life, even in her difficult relationship with Jacob? From a
human standpoint the marriage was initially a disaster. It was launched in deceit
and characterized by neglect. Yet from it came the most significant human
being ever to walk the face of the earth, Jesus of Nazareth.

Is it an overstatement to say that because Jacob and Leah stayed in their
marriage, troubled as it was, the course of human history was changed? Is it
going too far to say that because Leah trusted that God was at work in her life

and acknowledged His presence year after year, she became part of a plan that has shaken the world?

Let us say again, God has a higher and unseen purpose in our relationships than we can imagine. If we look at our husband or wife from a purely human standpoint, we can easily conclude it's pointless. And if it's a big mistake, why try to hang in there any longer? Why not fold our cards and leave the table? How many nights do we need to cry ourselves to sleep or fight back tears in the car, before admitting the marriage was a blunder and it's time to get out?

Let us suggest that maybe, just maybe, God has a bigger picture in mind for your life and marriage than you ever dreamed possible. But with few exceptions, that purpose won't be accomplished by choosing to give up and get out.

THE LESSONS OF JACOB AND LEAH'S STORY

What's remarkable about Leah is that she named Judah "Praise" when she had little or no idea how history was going to play itself out. But she knew there was a God in heaven who saw her suffering and misery in marriage. And rather than cashing in her relationship, she chose to go against her feelings and circumstances and trust God instead. Despite her pain, she found it in her soul to praise Him. And through her life we can draw several encouraging principles that apply to our marriages as well.

God is Bigger Than Our Bad Decisions

For the sake of discussion, let's assume you married someone that you now wish you had not married. Your marriage is strained, your spouse is distant, and your prospects for the future are looking grim. Are your life and marriage destined for nothing but unhappiness?

That's essentially a fatalist point of view. But fatalism is based on ancient pagan philosophy, not the teaching of Scripture. In fact, the Bible knows nothing of fatalism. The Scriptures hold out the hope that with God "all things are possible."[10] Over and over again the New Testament refers to God as "the God of all hope."[11]

The truth is, God's purposes are greater than our poor choices. He can accomplish things in our lives we never imagined, in spite of our mistakes. God can use imperfect people to accomplish his perfect will.

Go back to the family tree of Jesus as an example. The ancestry of Joseph and Mary reads in some cases like a soap opera. In the list of names you will discover adulterers, prostitutes, idol worshipers, and murderers.

Why would God print such embarrassing information about the family ancestry of Joseph and Mary? After all, this is the Bible. You would think God would have edited it more carefully. But those names are there deliberately to make the point that God specializes in using damaged goods to accomplish his purposes. The doctrine of grace teaches that God shows us his mercy and favor even when we've messed up or made some major bad choices. Our one bad choice is not the final word.

God Can Pick Us Up Right Where We Are

Perhaps you did marry someone over the objections or warning of family or friends. Perhaps you did get sexually involved too soon and now regret it. Or maybe you married someone because of your own insecurities, not because it was a good choice.

God knew you would do that even before you did. But even your bad decision is not beyond the scope of his power to take a wrong choice and use it for his purposes.

When we were in seminary, we met a pilot who had lived most of his early adult life in complete rebellion against God. His father bad been a minister, but when he died of a heart attack at a young age, the son became bitter and blamed God for taking his father from him. He was out to prove he didn't need that type of God.

After college he entered the Air Force. Both his lifestyle and goals made it clear he would do whatever he pleased with his life. That included the choice of a wife. She was a beautiful and gentle person, but she too had chosen to live as if God didn't exist.

He survived over two hundred combat missions in North Vietnam, narrowly escaping death several times. But his rebellion had exacted a high toll on his life. One Christmas Day sitting on the runway waiting to take of on another bombing mission, he suddenly thought, "What unfortunate series of decisions did I make that have put me in a place like this on Christmas?"

When he returned home, he and his wife underwent an amazing transformation. He discovered that the God he had attempted to run from had refused to let him get away. And he did something he thought he would never do again, not since the day his father died. He prayed and asked God to forgive him for living as a prodigal. He decided to trust Christ for his salvation and asked God to allow him a fresh start.

Once he completed his final tour of duty, he retired and entered seminary. For many years now he and his sweet wife have been used to encourage countless people as they've ministered in several churches throughout the Southeastern United States.

Was their getting married a mistake? They never consulted God or gave much thought to how things might turn out. Yet the Heavenly Father, who can see the end from the beginning, had a plan in mind for their lives.

Nothing about Your Life Is an Accident

God has a plan in mind for you as well. There is a purpose behind your existence and a reason for your being on earth at this time. Nothing about you is accidental. Nor is your marriage too big a problem for God to solve. It didn't catch him by surprise, nor has it foiled his plans for you to serve Him.

How can we be so sure? Well, can you imagine God pacing up and down the corridors of heaven, wringing his hands, muttering to himself, *What in the world am I going to do about Michael and Renee's marriage? I never saw it coming. What do I do now?* We can't.

If both of you are willing to take that leap of faith and believe that God is bigger than your doubts and current problems, you may begin to discover that higher and hidden purposes in your marriage. What you'll find is that He has been working in you life far longer than you ever realized. What seems at one time like a huge mistake may turn out to be part of a masterful plan.

God's Purposes Ultimately Prevail

Don't rush too soon into thinking your marriage is a meaningless relationship. The final chapter has not been written. You haven't seen everything God intends to do with your relationship. The Scriptures assure us, "So is my word that goes out from my mouth: It will not return to me empty, but will accomplish what I desire and achieve the purpose for which I sent it."[12]

What God has set out to do in your marriage He will accomplish. We urge you to look beyond your immediate circumstances and emotions and place your faith in the fact that God is working out something much higher and bigger than we can possibly imagine.

John and Vera Mae Perkins are remarkable people. Together they have started efforts in rural Mississippi to help people help themselves through food cooperatives, health clinics, and much more. When we were in school, we spent an entire month with them in Jackson, Mississippi, restoring homes to sell to neighbors at a reasonable price. And we observed firsthand the strength of their relationship.

But their marriage wasn't always a bed of roses. When they were first married, they experienced such tremendous strife that they separated. Both had come to the conclusion that their marriage was a mistake. To make matters worse, Vera Mae discovered she was pregnant.

For over a year they lived in separate parts of the nation, and the marriage looked doomed. Finally, Vera Mae's mother scrimped together enough money to send her daughter to California to see John and "get it settled," which most likely meant divorce.

But when Vera Mae stepped off the bus with their firstborn son in her arms, John Perkin's hard heart melted. After they decided not to divorce, God began working in their hearts. John had a dramatic spiritual experience that changed the course of their lives. They both experienced God's call to help others. Eventually that meant going back to Mississippi to try to alleviate the suffering of impoverished people.

They paid a high price for their concern. Once John was arrested by the highway patrol, taken to a local jail, and beaten within an inch of his life. Only his wife's brave efforts demanding his release saved him.

Later John and Vera Mae worked in the riot-torn neighborhoods of Los Angeles, trying to help broken families and a fractured culture. What a terrible shame if their marriage had come to a premature end years ago. So many people who needed their love and encouragement would have missed out. So much good would have gone undone. But God had a higher purpose for their lives than just "getting it settled." Today they serve as role models in their community, living witnesses of the fact that a "big mistake" can be transformed into a tremendous source of happiness and fulfillment.[13]

CONCLUSION

Are you ready to give up because you believe your marriage should never have been? The next time you attend a Christmas program with its stirring music and glorious message of a Savior born to the world, just remember that, in part, you have Jacob and Leah to thank. Leah didn't give up. She didn't choose the easy way out. She trusted that God knew what he was doing, and the world is still experiencing the results of her faith.

It may not be clear to you tomorrow, or even the next day, just what God is doing in your marriage. But if you choose to live by faith, rather than by circumstances or emotions, God will honor you and eventually give you a glimpse of His higher and hidden purposes. There's no telling what you may discover.

Chapter Twelve

PLAYING FOR KEEPS

SEVERAL OF US WERE PLAYING VOLLEYBALL outside on Saturday afternoon when we were interrupted by the noise of a wedding entourage. Horns were blaring, streamers were flying, and wedding attendants were waving at us as they cruised by in shining white limousines.

"You poor fool," the man next to us muttered, unaware that anyone was listening. "You have no idea what you're getting yourself into."

We gathered that his marriage had been less than satisfying.

If a couple doesn't get along well, or constantly feels dissatisfied, or frequently questions if they even love each other, can they start over? Is there a way to replace anger and unhappiness with love and intimacy? Yes, we believe there is a way back. It's found in what we call the Jacob and Leah Principle of Marriage. That principle simply states: Despite a bad start, God can bless your life together and give you a genuine love for each other.

"Wait a minute," you may be saying. "What evidence is there that Jacob and Leah ever developed a meaningful relationship?"

We're glad you asked. Genesis tells us that Jacob eventually decided to leave his crooked father-in-law's business. When he asked Leah and Rachel if they were willing to go with him, they both replied, "Do we still have any share in the inheritance of our father's estate?...So do whatever God has told you."[1] Despite all the hurt in Leah's life, when the moment arrived, she chose to cast her lot with her husband and leave her father behind.

After Jacob arrived in the land of Canaan, his wife Rachel died while giving birth to their second son, Benjamin. It was a devastating loss for Jacob, and he set up a pillar as a perpetual memorial over her grave. Apparently Leah outlived her sister by several more years.

Although Genesis is silent about the intervening time, we are told that decades later Leah died and a famine forced Jacob to move his family to Egypt to avoid starvation. As he reached the end of his life years later, he gathered his sons around him and made one final request. He did not want to be buried in Egypt,

so he tells them: "I am about to be gathered to my people. Bury me with my fathers in the cave in the field of Ephron the Hittite, the cave in the field of Machpelah, near Mamre in Canaan, which Abraham [his grandfather] bought as a burial place from Ephron the Hittite, along with the field. There Abraham and his wife Sarah were buried, there Isaac [his father] and his wife Rebekah were buried, and *there I buried Leah*."[2] The Scriptures then tell us, "When Jacob had finished giving instructions to his sons, he drew his feet up into the bed, breathed his last and was gathered to his people."[3]

We want the full significance of this story to sink into your soul. Jacob with his final breath asks his sons to bury him – next to Leah, not Rachel. In a culture that highly regarded the sanctity of tradition and family, Jacob reminded his sons that his grandparents were buried together, his parents were buried together, and that he now wished to be buried next to his wife Leah. The very fact he buried her in the ancestral plot and asked to be placed next to her is a profound statement of his honor and esteem for her at the end of his life. The fact he regarded Leah as belonging to the same category as his grandmother and mother suggests a deeper level of intimacy, bonding, and love for Leah that had finally taken root in his heart. Although he spent the majority of his life favoring Rachel and spurning Leah, in his final years he came to see his marriage to Leah as the legacy God had blessed. He accorded her the same honor given to Sarah and Rebekah, the beloved wives of Abraham and Isaac.

That's what we mean when we say God can change your mind about the person you married.

LEARNING TO TRUST
THE HEART OF GOD

Things that begin all wrong don't have to end that way. Marriage is not a straight-line graph. It may take some unexpected curves, but God can use them to bless your life together and give you a genuine love for one another. It was slow in coming, but sometime during Jacob's final years he saw that what began as a deception was actually no mistake at all. And, as history so dramatically records, his marriage to Leah was part of a glorious plan that produced David, Solomon, Joseph, Mary, and finally Jesus the Christ.

If God can heal a marriage such as Jacob and Leah's, why can't he do the same thing in your life? Why can't God take a heart of stone and replace it with a heart of tenderness toward your mate? Why can't He demonstrate to you that his plan for your life is much bigger and more magnificent than you have ever imagined? Why can't He reveal to you that he's been operating in your life long before you ever realized it?

That's why we say there's hope for marriages that begin all wrong or get way offtrack. Because there actually is. That hope is found in trusting God, who has revealed himself in Jesus Christ. The grace of God is available to every marriage because of the finished work of Christ on the cross. There, bearing our sins, he opened the way to a relationship with God that can literally transform our lives. As we recognize our need for forgiveness and reconciliation with God, the gift of grace is offered to us.

Simply tell God you accept the finished work of Christ on the cross. Ask for the gift of eternal life. "For it is by grace you have been saved, through faith—and this not from yourselves, it is the gift of God—not by works, so that no one can boast"[4]. Then thank Him for the free gift of your forgiveness and salvation.

As the Apostle Paul once wrote, "For the wages of sin is death, but the gift of God is eternal life in Christ Jesus our Lord"[5]. We don't have to attend a seminar, buy a CD series, or make an exotic pilgrimage to discover this healing grace. We simply have to ask and trust God for it.

The result is a new ability to love other people, particularly our husbands and wives. The Apostle John, often known as the Apostle of Love, wrote: "Dear friends, let us love one another, for love comes from God....This is love: not that we loved God, but that he loved us and sent his Son as an atoning sacrifice for our sins. Dear friends, since God so loved us, we also ought to love one another"[6].

The most effective way to ensure our marriage is for keeps is to turn to God. Through Jesus Christ he can give us a new love for our husband or wife. A fresh start in our relationship begins with a fresh start with God.

We read once of a couple who could never agree whether to listen to the news or classical music. After the wife began trusting in Christ's love, she surprised her husband one day by switching the remote to the news.

"Why did you do that?" he asked.

"Because I know it's what you like to listen to," she replied.

He turned it back to music. From that point on the acrimony and fighting in their marriage dissipated. Why? Because the love of God allowed them to go beyond themselves to show love to the other person.

FOUR STEPS
TO A FRESH START

Couples who want a fresh start in their marriage must make four important decisions.

1. Make a conscious decision before God to remain married to this person for the rest of your life.

Until we settle that issue once and for all, we will never experience a genuine fresh start. As long as we're still weighing our options, we'll never come home to our spouse. Our heart will always be elsewhere.

People in troubled relationships often fantasize to escape the difficult realities of their marriage. They see an attractive person and think, "I know I'd be happy with him (or her)." They refuse to invest the needed time and energy in their marriage because their thoughts are always with someone else.

Only when we stop such emotional window-shopping and decide to enjoy the purchase we made on our wedding day will our feelings begin to change. We need to say to ourselves, "If I'm to enjoy Venus for a wife, or Adonis for a husband, it will have to be the person I'm married to."

We attended a school banquet one evening where one of the men at the head of the table was flirting with a woman much younger than he was. He didn't realize that anyone else noticed, but he virtually ignored his wife and spent the entire night talking to and smiling at the other woman. Unless we are firmly committed to remaining married to our mate, we will become prisoners of perpetual distraction and may embarrass ourselves in front of others.

The good news is that human beings have an amazing ability to adapt. If we decide to be contented with the person we married, we will eventually feel that contentment.

For several years early in our marriage, we drove a car that we called our "After-Dinner Mint." It earned that name because the manufacturer painted it a yellow-green combination, the colors found in the chocolate mint wafers you buy at the checkout counter.

It ran well, needed few major repairs, and at five hundred dollars was a steal. But the color was such an embarrassment that our children didn't want to be seen in it.

Around town we received a number of dirty looks from other drivers, implying everything from, "I suppose you wear matching polyester pants," to "You know the EPA has outlawed cars like yours." Our self-esteem took a number of hits as we cruised around Chicago in our yellow-green car.

But when we sat down and added up the cost of buying another car complete with tax, title, insurance, and stickers, the After-Dinner Mint always looked much better to us. When we finally sold it, it was an emotional loss for all of us.

Obviously relationships are a much more serious matter than used cars. And learning to be content with another person is a much more complex task than getting used to an old automobile. But it is true that once we decide to be satisfied with what we have, we can find a spirit of delight. To renew a marriage, both individuals need to say before God, "I choose this day to remain married to this person for the rest of my life and will not even consider any other alternatives."

2. Choose to make your marriage the most important relationship in your life.

That means putting your husband or wife above your relationship with your relatives, parents, co-workers, and even children. Our order of priorities must be God first, our spouse second, our children third, and then others.

A friend in the military once told us that when he would return from active duty overseas he would first meet his wife for a day alone, leaving the children with a baby-sitter. Then he would come home and greet his children. That's the kind of priority we need to give our husbands or wives. Our relationship with our spouse needs to take precedence over time spent on the phone with our friends and relatives, a round of golf played with clients, and commitments to even worthwhile causes.

Chuck Swindoll once commented that he's attended more than one funeral where the husband wept on his shoulder and said, "I never knew what I really had until she was gone." Don't let that happen in your life. Don't wait until it's too late to make your marriage the priority it needs to be.

How do you do that? How do people act toward the most important person in their life? They talk about that person frequently, think about him or her when they're away, and say no to other people just so they can spend time together. Choosing to make our marriage our top priority relationship may seem awkward at first. The emotional satisfaction may not be strong right away. But the more time and attention both partners invest in the relationship, the more that will change.

Have you ever noticed the difference in your sexual attraction to each other when you're away alone together for an unhurried evening versus when you're cooking supper at 5:00 o'clock on a Tuesday night? For romance and courtship to flourish, you need to recreate the conditions of your dating years, time alone, time to talk, time to laugh. Couples choosing to work split shifts, two jobs, or weekends aren't giving their relationship a chance. It may call for a drastic change in your standard of living or a new job or revised budget, but if the marriage is going to survive, you have to see each other for at least fifteen hours a week.

It may also mean telling your relatives that your husband or wife comes first. Many well-meaning in-laws simply assume they have the same priority in their children's lives they once did. It can't work that way. Holidays, discretionary time, and vacations need to be considered first with our spouse's needs in mind. Both of you may agree that time should be spent with relatives, but your marriage comes first.

We also need to see our children in proper perspective. We are given them for only a few years. If our marriage has been made a top priority throughout those years, it will not only sustain us during the empty nest, it may thrive. But the time to be building that marriage is now, not when our last child graduates from high school or college.

Finally, we can't allow careers to disrupt our marriage. We need to remember that we work to live; we ought not to live to work. Individuals who spend their entire lives giving their best shot to the company often make a sad discovery. They've reached the top of the corporate ladder, but they have left their family behind. A successful business man once confessed he was not interested in participating in a heart disease reduction program at work. "Why would I want to live longer?" he said. "I have only a banking relationship with my family."

Choosing to make our marriage our first priority may be difficult. But we can get a fresh start only if we choose to truly "leave" all other relationships, to truly become "one" with our husband or wife.

3. Choose to act our love toward the other person.

We once heard a family seminar speaker make the profound statement, "Love is action." He was right. Essentially love is how we act toward other people.

We have many all-talk radio stations in Chicago. Twenty-four hours a day you can switch them on, and all you hear is talk. Seven days a week. Twelve months a year. Nothing but talk. It's far too easy for us as husbands or wives to be "all-talk radio" when it comes to loving our spouse. Love is not what we say, or what we intend to do, but what we actually do. A few years ago we bought some canned vegetables at a giant warehouse. I (Cheryl) was fixing supper a few nights later when upon seeing what I saw let out a hair-raising scream.

"What's wrong?" Bob asked, running into the kitchen.

"That's what's wrong," I said, pointing at the pan of vegetables on the stove. Right in the middle was a mouse—a dead mouse.

There are moments in a marriage when love has to go beyond talking to doing. Doing in this case meant carrying the pan and the mummified mouse outside and disposing of it. We both hesitated. This was no ordinary dirty job; this was a major league gross-out. We won't tell you who finally did the deed, but let's just say love can sometimes be costly.

There's no substitute for doing something that's loving. What's the alternative? To stay distant, to demand the other person make the first gesture, to spend our life in loneliness and isolation just to make a point?

Love is doing for the other person all the things our selfish human nature doesn't want to do. It's leaving the last slice of pizza for our beloved, spending time with their friends, and picking up the other person's dry cleaning on our way home from work. It's all the small ways we can say, "I love you more than I love me."

A Hollywood celebrity once claimed that the most important person in life ought to be ourselves. Ultimately, she said, we spend all day with ourselves, we eat with ourselves, we go to bed with ourselves. Her remarks fit the narcissistic spirit of the age, but they are pathetically misinformed. If the most important person in our lives is ourselves, we will never know true love or intimacy. Only in giving our lives away do we discover the secret of living and loving. Someone illustrated the difference between heaven and hell by saying that heaven is a place where people are eager to serve, while everyone waits to be served in hell. (Of course we know hell will be much worse than that.)

If we can put aside the cult of Self that has become enthroned in the last decades and ask what it really means to love another person, we'll discover it is often doing the hard thing. It's giving up our wants, our wishes, our personal goals in favor of blessing the life of another person.

4. Choose to believe that God
has an extraordinary plan for your marriage.

We want to close this book by emphasizing that nothing ever catches God by surprise. No event in our lives, no trauma, no heartache, no disappointment escapes His notice or catches him off guard. He is not the author of sin and suffering, but he is the Master of all things. That's why He has the ability to take the worst moments of our lives and give them meaning.

If anyone should know the truth of that statement, it is our friend Marshall Shelley. Marshall and his wife, Susan, lost two children within three months. The first was a boy, Toby, who died two minutes after birth due to congenital birth defects. A few months later, their two-year-old daughter, Mandy, who had been born with a brain condition that left her sightless, speechless, and deaf, died of pneumonia.

But before Mandy died, she had made a powerful impression on others. A hospital employee walked into Mandy's room and said to Marshall and his wife, "I've known for some time that I've needed to get God into my life, but it never seemed to be the right time or place. I'd like you to help me get God into my life, because every time I walk by her room, I see angels hovering over her crib."

A family in Marshall's church told them that their young son had always refused to pray until he heard Mandy was sick. That night he prayed his first prayer.

A hospital volunteer, supposedly sent to comfort the family, ended up pouring out the story of her divorce, remarriage, and alienation from God. In Mandy's presence, she felt like God was real to her again.

A man in their congregation wrote the Shelleys after Mandy's death, saying, "I never held Mandy, though I occasionally stroked her cheek while my wife held her. But I learned a lot from her. You've probably seen me standing by myself against the wall in the church lobby. I don't talk to many people. I feel like an empty well. I don't have much to say. But if God can use someone like Mandy, maybe he can use an empty well like me."

Marshall and Susan have come to believe that God can take our most painful situations and transform them into something precious and meaningful. "Could a sightless, wordless, helpless infant ever be a 'successful human being'? If success is fulfilling God's purposes, I consider Mandy wildly successful," her father later wrote.[7]

If God can accomplish His purposes in Mandy's life, can He not do the same in your life and mine? He is willing to take us just as we are, with all our weaknesses and problems, and accomplish some magnificent purpose for our lives and marriage.

PLAY FOR KEEPS

Bob never met his grandmother, Eva Moeller. She died on the dusty and lonely plains of a western prairie state when his father was just seventeen years old. Yet his father credits her with pointing him toward God at an early age. So profound was her impact on his life that at her graveside he vowed never to do anything that would dishonor her memory.

Apart from that, we knew little about her until many summers ago when we attended a large family reunion in the Midwest. Sitting across the table from us was a relative of Bob's father. We decided to ask her about Bob's grandmother, now gone for over fifty years.

She looked a bit nervous and then said, "Don't tell anyone I told you this."

Now we were more than a little curious. "Certainly, what is it?" Bob said.

"As far as we know, your grandmother was a mail-order bride," she said. "Your grandfather was a bachelor, homesteading on the prairie where there were very few women. We believe she must have answered an advertisement to come West."

When Bob later relayed the information to his sisters, they filled in a part of the story he had never heard. As his grandfather was dying, he asked everyone to leave the room except Bob's two oldest sisters. His grandfather was then eighty-nine and had been a widower for nearly thirty years.

"Do you know why I never remarried?" he asked in a raspy voice.

The two girls shook their heads no.

"Because when your grandmother died, I realized I could never love another woman as much as I loved her."

We tell this story to make a point. If indeed Bob's grandfather and grandmother began their marriage through a mail-order arrangement and yet learned to love each other that deeply, who's to say God can't do something just as extraordinary in your marriage?

If, like Jacob and Leah, you started out all wrong, who's to say God can't use your relationship to bless not only your lives but future generations as well?

Who's to say your marriage hasn't been in the plan of God from eternity past?

Why not begin your fresh start today? All of heaven is on your side. Christ himself wants you to succeed. You have nothing to lose but your unhappiness and despair. You have everything to gain—including glorifying God and the joy of falling in love.

Take the chance to start all over again. And may the God of all hope be with you both.

NOTES

Chapter One: Not According to Plan

1. Lawrence Kurdek, "The Relations between Well-being and Divorce History, Availability of a Proximate Adult, and Gender," *Journal of Marriage and the Family* 53 : 71-78.

Chapter Two: Checking In at Heartbreak Hotel

1. Genesis 29:21-27.
2. Ibid., 30.
3. Ibid., 32.
4. Ibid., 33.
5. Ibid., 34.
6. Proverbs 31:30
7. Anastasia Toufexis, "The Right Chemistry," *Time* 141, no. 7 : 49-51.
8. Alfred DeMaris and Vaninadha Rao, "Premarital Cohabitation and Subsequent Marital Stability in the United States: A Reassessment," *Journal of Marriage and the Family* 54, no. 1: 178-90.
9. Frank Furstenberg, "Bringing Back the Shotgun Wedding," *Public Interest* 90 : 121-27.

Chapter Three: Searching for the Escape Clause

1. Arland Thorton, "Changing Attitudes toward Family Issues in the United States," *Journal of Marriage and the Family* 51: 873-93.
2. Matthew 19:3-6.
3. Leslie Morgan, "Economic Well-being Following Marital Termination: A Comparison of Widowed and Divorced Women," *Journal of Family Issues* 10 : 86-101.
4. "Breaking the Divorce Cycle," *Newsweek* : 48.
5. Ibid., 49.
6. Ibid.
7. Proverbs 5:15-17.
8. Ibid., 6:27-29.
9. Ibid., 32-33
10. Bob Moeller, "When Your Children Pay the Price," *Leadership Journal* 14, no. 2: 86-95.
11. Proverbs 5:18-19.
12. William Willimon, "Risky Business," *Christianity Today*: 24-25.
13. Elizabeth Thomas and Ugo Collela, "Cohabitation and Marital Stability: Quality or Commitment," *Journal of Marriage and the Family* 54, no. 2: 759-67.
14. Willimon, "Risky Business," 24.

15. Robert Lauer et al., "The Long-term Marriage: Perceptions of Stability and Satisfaction," *International Journal of Aging and Human Development* 31, no. 3: 189-95.

Chapter Four: If You Keep Your Vows, They'll Keep You
1. Lesley Dormen, "The Five Turning Points of Love," *Glamour*: 192.
2. Ibid., 192-193.
3. Matthew 19:4-7.
4. "My Problem: I Was Still in Love with My Ex-husband," *Good Housekeeping*: 26-27.
5. Matthew 22:37-39.
6. 1 Corinthians 13:4-7.
7. Quoted in "Secrets of Staying Together," *Reader's Digest*: 152.
8. Ibid., 154.
9. Bob Moeller, "What If Beer Ads Lasted Longer than 60 Seconds?" *Focus on the Family*, 11.
10. Ecclesiastes 2:10-11.

Chapter Six: Communication Is the Key
1. Lois Leiderman Davitz, Ph.D., "Why Men Divorce," *McCall's*: 26.
2. Ibid., 26, 30.
3. Ibid., 30.
4. Norman Shawchuck, *How to Manage Conflict in the Church: Understanding and Managing Conflict.* 2 vols. (Indianapolis: Spiritual Growth Resources, 23-25, and Kenneth Thomas, *The Handbook of Industrial and Organizational Psychology*, vol. 2.
5. Scott Winokur, "What Happy Couples Do Right," *Redbook* : 66.
6. Ibid.

Chapter Seven: Aren't My Needs Your Needs?
1. Robert, Michael et al., *Sex in America: A Definitive Survey* (Boston: Little, Brown and Company, 1994), 93.
2. Ibid, 116.
3. Lois Leiderman Davits, Ph.D., "Why Men Divorce," *McCall's* no. 26.
4. Jimmy Evans, *Marriage on the Rock* (New York: McCrecken Press, 1994).

Chapter Nine: You Can't Have It All
1. Genesis 30:14-16.
2. Dolf Zillman and Jennings Bryant, "Effect of Prolonged Consumption of Pornography on Family Values," *Journal of Family Issues* 9, no. 4: 518-44.
3. "The War Within," *Leadership Journal* 8, no. 4 : 97-112.

4. I Corinthians 7:4.4. I Corinthians 7:4.

Chapter Eleven: The Higher and Hidden Purposes of God
1. Genesis 29:32-33; 30:17, 19-20 (italics added by authors).
2. Ibid., 29:35.
3. Ibid., 3:15.
4. Ibid., 12:3.
5. Ibid., 28:14.
6. Ibid., 49:1-10.
7. 2 Samuel 2:4 (italics added by authors).
8. Luke 1:26-33 (italics added by authors).
9. Ibid., 3:23-38 (italics added by authors).
10. Matthew 19:26.
11. Romans 15:13.
12. Isaiah 55:11.
13. Vera Mae Perkins, "How I Stayed Married for 40 Years." *Urban Family* pt. 1, 1, no. 3: 28-29.

Chapter Twelve: Playing for Keeps
1. Genesis 31:14.
2. Ibid., 49:29-32 (italics added by author).
3. Ibid., 33.
4. Ephesians 2:8-9.
5. Romans 6:23.
6. I John 4:7, 10.
7. Marshall Shelley, "The Sightless, Wordless Theologian," *Christianity Today* 37, no. 5: 34-36.

MarriageVine is a biblical organization with a vision to see marriages succeed.

Our Mission:

MarriageVine exists to help cultivate growing marriages through resources, emails, websites, and events.

www.MarriageVine.com